AN OVERVIEW OF:

UNDERSTANDING MORALITY: QUESTS FOR THE GOOD LIFE

by

Wayne Gustave Johnson

Publisher: Wipf and Stock, 2022, Eugene, Oregon

(My) Broad Theory: *Normative ethical systems are best understood as attempts to seek out and justify ways of living a fulfilled human life in terms of the kind of fulfillment one believes to be possible given one's beliefs about human nature and the ultimate nature of all things. Furthermore, any normative ethical system must also indicate just how one's own quest for fulfillment is related to the experiences of other people and sentient beings, given, again, one's view of human nature and the ultimate nature of all things. In short, I claim that any normative ethical system must suggest a pathway to human fulfillment and must also indicate just how one's own fulfillment is related to other beings who also seek their fulfillment.* (p. 11)

SOME RELATED CLAIMS:

1. All major moral theories—religious or non-religious—claim that their

Understanding Morality

Understanding Morality

Quests for the Good Life

Wayne Gustave Johnson

WIPF & STOCK · Eugene, Oregon

UNDERSTANDING MORALITY
Quests for the Good Life

Copyright © 2022 Wayne Gustave Johnson. All rights reserved. Except for brief quotations in critical publications or reviews, no part of this book may be reproduced in any manner without prior written permission from the publisher. Write: Permissions, Wipf and Stock Publishers, 199 W. 8th Ave., Suite 3, Eugene, OR 97401.

Wipf & Stock
An Imprint of Wipf and Stock Publishers
199 W. 8th Ave., Suite 3
Eugene, OR 97401

www.wipfandstock.com

PAPERBACK ISBN: 978-1-6667-3017-3
HARDCOVER ISBN: 978-1-6667-2132-4
EBOOK ISBN: 978-1-6667-2133-1

01/19/22

To my children:
Susan, Scott, Jeffrey, Jonathan
And
To Marge

Contents

Introduction | 1
Chapter 1: A Theory About Moral Theories | 5
Chapter 2: The Point of Morality | 20
Chapter 3: Beyond Morality: Meaning and Significance | 30
Chapter 4: Moral Theories and Worldviews | 46
Chapter 5: Religion-based Morality | 97
Chapter 6: Self, Others, and Rights | 110
Chapter 7: Why Be Moral? | 127
Chapter 8: Ethical Relativism | 145
Chapter 9: The Free Will Problem | 154
Chapter 10: Evolution and Ethics | 162

Endnotes | 177
Bibliography | 183
Index | 189

Introduction

Philosophers generally agree that human beings quite naturally and appropriately seek a fulfilling life of some kind. In the quest for a fulfilling life, human beings find themselves in contact with others who also seek a fulfilling life. These quests are often mutually supportive as in family and friendship relations. These quests, however, are also often in conflict. The fulfillment of Joe may come at some cost to Jill. The conflicts involved in these mutual quests provide the setting for the development of moral systems of some kind. People seek a moral pathway which can promise not only fulfillment for the moral person but also an answer to the question of possible moral responsibility toward others. A "good life" is sought in both the non-moral sense—as in a "good" auto—and in the moral sense of good—as in that was a "good" deed. Over centuries, a variety of moral systems and guidelines which address this quest for a good life have developed. However, significant disagreements about these guidelines and systems persist. Morality seems to be a perennial scene for debate, and agreement about matters moral seems difficult to achieve.

This book will not attempt to give moral advice. While some views will be challenged in chapter 7, it will not argue for the validity or truth of any particular moral system. Instead, this book aims at helping the reader explore the nature of moral systems by explaining why these systems develop and why they differ so sharply. The author hopes that these attempts at explanation will clarify the nature of moral decisions and help the reader explore and confirm their own individual moral convictions.

This book may not make the search for a moral pathway easier since it suggests that moral decisions are both inevitable and numerous. However,

UNDERSTANDING MORALITY

following Søren Kierkegaard, it may be fruitful, at times, to make life decisions more difficult. Moral pathways are serious choices.

Since this book claims to explain the very nature of morality, it would seem appropriate to begin by posing possible moral issues. These issues will serve as background for the wider discussion of matters moral pursued in the book. Some issues are specific in nature, such as those raised by a variety of trolley problems that explore the choice of killing or letting die.[1]

Problem one: An empty runaway trolley is moving down a track. On the track ahead a dozen people are congregated and are unaware of the coming trolley. You are near a switch that could turn the trolley down a spur where only one person stands in danger. You apparently have the choice of either killing one person or letting a number of other persons die. Do you have a moral responsibility to throw the switch in order to save a number of lives even though one person will die because of your action? Are you morally prohibited from throwing that switch?

Problem two: An empty runaway trolley is moving down a track. On the track ahead a dozen people are congregated and are unaware of the danger. You are standing near a fat man. If you push the fat man onto the track his size will stop the trolley. This action will save a number of lives, but the fat man will die. Are you morally obligated to push the fat man onto the rails? Are you morally prohibited from doing so?

The above examples seem not to involve your own long-range self-interests, aside from any moral praise or blame you may receive. The problems can be altered so that your own long-range self-interests are deeply involved. Problem three: You are standing, alone, on the bank of a swollen river when you notice that a small child had fallen into the stream and could not swim. You are not a strong swimmer. Do you have a moral obligation to attempt to rescue the child at some risk to your own life? What if it were your child? Problem four: You have a comfortable lifestyle and income. You learn that small children are starving in another country. Do you have a moral obligation to help feed those children? If so, how much of your own resources should you give to that cause? Problem five: There are homeless people in your community, and the nights are cold. You own the house in which you live and have some spare bedrooms. Are you morally obligated to take in such a homeless person? Does it matter who this person might be? What if the homeless person is your child?

These last three issues may arouse a possible sense of guilt. If this is so, what is the nature of that guilt? Is it real guilt in the sense that you actually

INTRODUCTION

do have moral responsibilities in these situations? Or is it neurotic guilt as a feeling of guilt where there is no actual guilt? Or is it existential guilt in the sense that life by its nature lays moral burdens upon you which can only be borne, not remedied?[2]

On the other hand, the problems raised above may not have prompted any feeling of moral guilt for you. This would imply that you have reasons for not feeling guilt. Such reasons would represent a moral theory that justifies your lack of a feeling of guilt. How would you formulate such a theory?

A summary of the following chapters follows. Chapter 1 will set forth a Broad Theory about moral theories and explore the various phenomena that this Broad Theory seeks to explain, such as why there are so many competing moral theories and why agreement seems difficult to attain. Chapter 2 examines the point of morality. Why do moral systems develop at all? I will conclude, following William James, that moral reflection and moral systems are attempts to find a way to appropriately arbitrate among the competing wants, needs, and desires (WNDs) of human beings as well as other sentient creatures. These competing WNDs illustrate the conflicts that can develop in mutual quests for the good life. The challenging moral issues arise when both resources and human sympathies are limited.

In seeking to arbitrate among these competing WNDs, two related issues must be considered. The first issue is deciding which of *my own* WNDs should be honored? I cannot "eat my cake and have it too." This is the question of what constitutes a truly fulfilling human life. This fulfillment can be expressed in a variety of terms: happiness, pleasure, flourishing, excellence, peace, eternal glory. All major moral systems—religious or non-religious—address this question, and all assert that the quest for a fulfilled life is natural and legitimate. Furthermore, these systems also claim that the proposed moral pathway is necessarily part of the quest for fulfillment. Morality is "for us." Chapter 3 explores how the quest for the good life includes the quest for meaning and significance in the face of mortality and finitude. Chapter 4 presents brief summaries of significant moral theories put forward by a variety of philosophers. These summaries will trace how differing worldviews result in differing answers regarding the question of a fulfilling life and the question of moral responsibility. I seek to show that ontology matters. The fulfilling life proposed by Epicurus, for instance, is in sharp contrast to the view of a fulfilling life presented by Thomas Aquinas.

The second issue related to the task of arbitrating among competing WNDs is that of possible moral obligation toward others. In our quest for fulfillment, what view should we take regarding others who also seek a fulfilling life? Chapter 6 explores the concepts of justice and human rights while Chapter 7 examines possible moral obligations toward others.

Chapter 5 explores in some detail the nature of religion—based morality in its variety of forms. The chapter is purely descriptive and does not seek to defend or attack religion—based morality.

Chapter 7 explores the central question of "Why be moral?" In the quest for fulfillment, does a human being have any moral obligation to aid others even at some cost to the long-range fulfillment of their own life? This chapter also examines the theory of psychological egoism, which maintains that all deliberate human choices are basically motivated by self-interest.

Chapter 8 reviews the conflict between ethical absolutism and ethical relativism. Is it possible to rationally defend a particular moral system that appropriately applies to all human beings at any place and time? If not, do moral systems merely reflect the generally accepted moral views held by persons in any particular culture?

Chapter 9 explores the conflict between those who hold to freedom of the will and determinists who argue that all choices are caused. If determinism is true, would it be rational to hold persons morally responsible for their caused actions?

Finally, Chapter 10 considers whether or not evolutionary theory can provide something like moral insight. If genes dictate our eye color and sex, can they also determine our choices and actions? Can science show us what is moral? Should questions about morality be turned over to scientists, not philosophers and theologians?

This book is ambitious in that I seek to present a compelling overview of the nature of morality and the construction of moral systems and codes. On the other hand, however, this book is modest in that I present no compelling answer to moral problems. My hope is that this book will contribute to earnest discussion and dialogue about moral theories generally as well as specific moral issues. While sometimes distinctions are made between the terms "ethics" and "morality," I will be using the terms synonymously.

1

A Theory about Moral Theories

Though in theory we might think that a people could construct a wholly autonomous value system independent of any metaphysical reference, an ethics without ontology, we do not in fact seem to have found such a people.

—Clifford Geertz[3]

There does seem to be some connection between anthropology and ethics, that is, between what it is believed that man is and what it is believed that he ought to do.

—W. D. Hudson[4]

Human beings throughout history have been in quest of the good life. They have sought the "good" life in the sense of a happy or fulfilling life. Some human beings—but not all—have also sought the "good" life in the sense of a properly moral life. Much of human history can be seen as an attempt to harmonize these two quests. Is it possible, however, to bring those two quests into harmony? Is it possible to have a life that is both fulfilling and morally sound? Or may a commitment to a moral pathway obstruct the road to a fulfilling life?

In their quest for the good life, human beings also sought to understand the basic nature of the world in which their quest is lived out.

Attempts to understand the nature of the world can be roughly divided between religious worldviews and non-religious worldviews. While religious worldviews have tended to dominate human societies, there have long been voices in support of a vision of the world without any meaningful God, gods, or deities. Nevertheless, both worldviews involve a quest for the good life (happy, fulfilled) by those who hold that worldview. This analysis leads to basic questions: How do worldviews shape the pathway leading to the good life in both the moral and the non-moral sense? Does the morally good life entailed by a religious worldview differ from the morally good life proposed by a non-religious worldview? In more technical terms, are moral visions shaped by ontological or metaphysical commitments? This book proposes a theory about moral theories that aims to answer just such questions.

Worldviews

Since the role of worldviews is central to the analysis and argument that is to follow, some clarification of their nature and function should be offered. To hold a worldview is to possess a web or system of beliefs that constitute an understanding of the nature of the universe and of the human venture. Traditional religions represent such worldviews, as do various non-religious systems. Typical contemporary worldviews would include beliefs established through science. A worldview, however, is more than a mental picture of the empirical universe; it also encompasses what William James (1842–1910) called "overbeliefs" about the ultimate nature of reality and about what is meaningful or valuable. For James the empiricist, these matters are "overbeliefs" since they are neither justified nor entailed by empirical evidence. Nevertheless, James claimed all of us necessarily hold a variety of such overbeliefs that, true or false, function as basic guidelines for our goals and ventures. Beliefs are rules for actions.

Central to the nature of such overbeliefs, and consequently central to the nature of worldviews, is the question of whether or not anything exists above, beyond, or prior to the physical universe. In the history of philosophy this constitutes a fundamental ontological issue regarding the nature of being. Our Western cultural traditions provide us mainly with a choice between two worldviews—theism (or some modified form of such) or naturalism. Both are theories in the sense that they are conceptual constructs designed to explain aspects of our experience just as scientific theories attempt to explain natural phenomena. Theism and naturalism can be thought of as conceptual maps which serve as explanatory systems—as basic beliefs used to explain and interpret our world of experience as well as to ascertain what is valuable and guide our actions.

Theistic Worldview

The most common forms of theism in our culture are expressed in three related religions—Judaism, Christianity, and Islam. Those who fall into this camp believe that God (Yahweh, Allah) is the ultimate ground of all existence. God is eternal, non-material, beyond space and time, and all-powerful. This God brought the universe into being out of nothing, *ex nihilo*, and sustains the universe and all its inhabitants. Furthermore, according to this worldview, the history of the universe and of humanity moves toward some ultimate and glorious culmination under the guidance of the Divine Power. Because we are created by this God and are called into relationship with our Creator, our lives are meaningful and significant. Obedience to the Divine Will promises to lead us to the highest form of human fulfillment. The journey through this world may be troubled and dark at times, but the promise of fulfillment and various gifts of grace keep us from despair during our earthly journey.

The worldview just described is, of course, traditional theistic religion. For several decades, there has been a curious shift in beliefs as various individuals claim to be "spiritual" but not "religious." Since the meaning of this spirituality is so amorphous and vague, it seems best not to venture into that particular arena. Instead, traditional religious positions will be used for reference purposes and illustrations. While these positions may or may not be accurate worldviews, at least they provide a fairly clear idea of their meaning and structure.

Naturalism as a Worldview

Naturalism is the major alternative to theism as a worldview in our culture. An increasingly live option for persons, naturalism is the theory that only nature exists—only the universe and the physical realities contained therein. There is no God or similar reality, and nothing beyond, prior to, within, or under nature. To put the matter in a slightly different way, naturalism is usually an expression of ontological materialism, a philosophical theory asserting that matter—or matter/energy—is the fundamental, uncreated reality and the basis for all existing entities. This should properly be seen as a philosophical theory rather than a scientific theory since the claim runs beyond what scientific method can, in principle, pursue. Most modern forms of naturalism hold that nature is made up of forces and particles that can be studied by physics and that bring forth living creatures through the process of evolution. Evolution within a naturalistic worldview is usually seen as a random process with no particular aim and certainly no divine guiding hand in control. Nature does what it does according to the causal structures described by natural laws that explain the workings of natural processes.

Naturalism, then, implies that our human life is the product of a causal universe ordered by natural laws and acting through a random evolutionary process. Human beings are wholly physical entities with no separate reality such as mind or soul that lives within or parallel to the physical body. Consciousness and its various activities—such as thinking, feeling, remembering, choosing, and reading—are phenomena generated by the physical brain. We do not *have* bodies; we *are* bodies. When the body dies and the life processes cease, our consciousness shuts down and our bodies return to a more basic form of matter. There is no personal life possible beyond the death of the body. The meaning or point of our lives—if there is one—is to be found within the physical universe during the limited years of our individual existence.

Does "God" Make a Difference?

With this brief explanation of worldviews in place, I now return to the question of whether religious worldviews make a difference, for good or for ill. Does some notion of God or Divine Reality make a difference? Many voices of the past would answer this question with a resounding "Yes." These voices would include not only religious thinkers but also atheists and agnostics. Influential theologians in the Christian tradition have long argued that human reason, on its own, can neither grasp moral truth nor provide the motivation needed for the moral pathway. Philosophically inclined theologians, as Augustine (354–430) and Thomas Aquinas (1225–74), always appeal to revealed truth in the form of Scripture to anchor their final vision of morality. Martin Luther (1483–1546) and John Calvin (1509–64), the major Protestant reformers, were convinced that human beings are turned in upon themselves and blind to moral truth. Without grace-enabled faith, persons could neither see the good nor find the motivation to do the good.

A THEORY ABOUT MORAL THEORIES

On the other hand, many non-theistic philosophers have argued that belief in God does make a difference, but any morality based on religion fails both rationally and morally. Plato (429?–347 BCE), for example, held that the gods presented in Greek mythology were basically corrupt and should not serve as role models for the young. In his later works, however, Plato employed a view of God that supported his own moral theory. Contrary to Plato, his student Aristotle (384–322 BCE) constructed an ethical theory that is still influential but had nothing of significance to say about the role that gods might play. Furthermore, Epicurus (341–270 BCE), while he thought that gods might exist, held that they are irrelevant to our moral quest and that we should, as mere mortal creatures, pursue pleasure for the self.

Other thinkers have leveled harsh judgments against a morality that is rooted in the religious traditions. While proclaiming that "God is dead," Nietzsche (1844–1900) also dismissed Christian morality as a form of slave morality adopted by the weak and cowardly. Other more contemporary philosophers share, in part, Nietzsche's view. Richard Taylor "repudiates the debilitating egalitarianism of modern ethics" [and its religious roots] "in favor of the ideals of the ancient pagan moralists."[5] The late John Mackie takes a more moderate position. He held that, if true, the theistic position could make a significant difference to moral philosophy. But he argues that the theistic position has little by way of cogent argument to support it and that it remains largely incoherent. Hence, human beings must invent morality.[6] The more recent vigorous voice of Sam Harris has attacked religious faith, generally, as well the morality too often expressed in faith traditions. In its place, Harris seeks to ground a rational morality rooted in our scientific understanding of nature and human beings.[7]

By way of clarification, I will not claim that belief in God is necessary for living a morally decent life. Little empirical evidence would support such a claim. Nor will I attempt to defend or defeat religious worldviews and the moral systems linked to them. No moral advice will be given. Instead, I will seek to develop a theory that acknowledges and clarifies the differences between religious and naturalistic moral theories and also explains *why* these differences occur. Instead of critiquing standard moral theories or developing and defending one in particular, a general theory *about* such moral theories will be offered.

On Facts and Theories

While no detailed analysis of the nature and role of theories will be developed here, some basic characteristics will be noted. At this point, a common distinction between "fact" and "theory" will be helpful. This distinction is reflected in everyday use of language. While it seems appropriate to speak of a theory as being either true or false (adequate or inadequate), it would be odd to speak of a false fact. Of course, a belief that some X is a fact may be a false belief; but the claim that X is a fact implies the claim that X is true. The major distinction can be expressed as follows: A statement of fact is a statement about something directly presented to our sensory experience or about a logical relationship. Thus, it is a fact that when I drop a ball it falls to the ground. And it is a fact that two plus two equals four. On the other hand, a theory is not a statement about what is directly presented to us, but is, rather, a construct designed primarily to *explain* certain facts. We do not experience theories directly by way of our sensory faculties; we use theories to help us explain certain experiences. It may be a fact that my window is broken, but I will seek for a theory that could help explain that fact. While it is a *fact* that a ball drops to the ground when released from my hand, Newton's *theory* of gravity *explains* why the ball falls to the ground.

The main function of any theory is that of explaining certain events or states of affairs. When coroners, for instance, seek to ascertain the cause of someone's death, they develop a theory—based on the facts of the case—that will explain the cause of the death. Newton's theory (or law) of universal gravitation explains a variety of phenomena such as why a rock will return to the earth even when hurled upward into the air and why an apple falls down instead of up when it breaks from a branch. When a physician prescribes a treatment, she is acting on a theory related to the factual observations obtained by the physical examination of her patient. It is clear, then, that theories are not to be taken lightly. To say of some theory that it is "only a theory" is to fail to see that most human actions are predicated on some theory that a particular person holds. We live by our theories; and sometimes we die because of them.

If the function of a theory is to explain certain phenomena, then it is successful to the degree that it explains phenomena relevant to that theory. Rather than developing an analysis of how theories do explain, or what constitutes an explanation of some fact by way of a theory (How does Newton's theory of gravitation explain why an apple falls to the earth?), the reader's own understanding of this matter will be accepted.

A THEORY ABOUT MORAL THEORIES

Some Facts to Be Explained

If my theory about ethical theories is to be successful, it must explain a variety of phenomena related to morality. The most significant phenomena to be explained include the following: 1) Fact: Human beings and human cultures tend to develop systems of morality or codes of ethics. What is there about the human situation that leads to such systems or codes? 2) Fact: Thoughtful human beings have generated a wide variety of views about the nature of morality. How can so much variety be explained? 3) Fact: It seems to be difficult if not impossible for all thoughtful people to come to agreement about moral principles and rules. What accounts for this difficulty? 4) Fact: Religion-based moral systems often have a substantially different view of morality than do non-religious systems. What accounts for these differences?

A Broad Theory *about* Moral Systems

At this point, I present what I shall call my "Broad Theory" formulated to explain the various facts listed above. Following the formulation of that Broad Theory, I will state four basic claims linked to it. No defense of the theory or the basic claims will be made in this chapter, but the remainder of this work will serve as such a defense.

Broad Theory: *Normative ethical systems are best understood as attempts to seek out and justify ways of living a fulfilled human life in terms of the kind of fulfillment one believes to be possible given one's beliefs about human nature and the ultimate nature of all things. Furthermore, any normative ethical system must also indicate just how one's own quest for fulfillment is related to the experiences of other people and sentient beings, given, again, one's view of human nature and the ultimate nature of all things.* In short, I claim that any normative ethical system must suggest a pathway to human fulfillment and must also indicate just how one's own fulfillment is related to other beings who also seek their fulfillment.

Two clarifications are in order. A normative ethical system is one that sets forth and defends certain moral norms as the correct ones to be adopted and followed. Such systems differ from a descriptive approach to ethics that would describe moral views held by people but would not attempt to support a specific set of principles. An anthropologist may, for example, describe the moral views held by certain groups of people, but would not, as anthropologist, propose that some such moral views are to be adopted and others rejected. By beliefs about the "ultimate nature of things," I have in mind certain metaphysical beliefs or ontological commitments, such as ontological materialism, naturalism, or a kind of transcendentalism or theism—that is, some type of worldview.

Claims Linked to the Broad Theory

Four basic claims are linked to this Broad Theory: 1) The principle aim of any rationally justifiable moral theory is to identify life pathways that will result in a fulfilling existence for anyone walking that pathway. "Fulfilling," here, remains intentionally vague. The same point could be made by substituting "flourishing" for "fulfilling." I have deliberately avoided the term "happiness" as the most basic aim of a rational person even though a number of important voices have used that term. While happiness is a significant dimension of human experience, it strikes me as too superficial or unsubstantial to qualify universally as the most fulfilling of life's quest.

The Role of Sanctions

One implication follows from this first claim. If the principal aim of a moral theory is to identify a pathway that leads to fulfillment, then that moral theory would also claim that straying from the moral pathway would in some way hinder or undercut the fulfillment of the one who so strays. In short, every moral theory includes some theory of sanctions such that failure to live morally leads inescapably to lack of fulfillment. Sanctions, of course, can take many forms. In traditional Western theism, moral failure can be sanctioned by either temporary or eternal punishment. In Far Eastern thought, the sanctions are applied through the working out of the Law of Karma and various forms of reincarnation. For Epicurus, the sanction would be that of failing to experience the life of pleasure; while for Aristotle, ethical failure would entail failing to be a truly excellent man. Or perhaps moral failure leads to a sense of personal disgust with one's own life—"Am I really that kind of person?" Any attempt to remove sanctions from a moral theory would, it appears, strip it of its human seriousness. Without sanctions of some kind, moral requirements might be interesting but trivial.

Normative ethical theories differ largely because of differing metaphysical commitments or worldviews held by the theorist. These commitments determine, in part, beliefs about what kind of fulfillment is possible, given the nature of things.

Normative moral theories differ also in part because of various views regarding the question of how other human beings (or other sentient creatures), in their quest for fulfillment, are related to one's own quest. Some persons (or creatures) matter for us because their fulfillment is intimately related to our own. Others do not count in the same way.

The substance of a morality rooted in theistic religious traditions cannot be defended successfully on non-theistic or naturalistic foundations. Since many theists as well as atheists assent to this claim, it implies neither an endorsement nor a rejection of a religion-based morality.

Clarifications

I need, now, to guard against a possible misinterpretation. My theory is not to be construed as a defense of certain positions declared in the current culture war; nor is it to be understood as a claim that moral degradation must inevitably follow from the demise of religious belief. Any such implication or claim would run far beyond the *descriptive* intent of my theory. I give no advice and make no judgments in this work. Consequently, the adequacy of a morality rooted in a theistic worldview or one rooted in a naturalistic worldview will remain an open question.[8]

Since my theory attempts to explain a variety of facts about morality and historical ethical theories, two important distinctions often made in moral philosophy will need to be clarified. If the Broad Theory is to be successful, it must be able to explain not only the facts cited earlier, but also the bases for the two distinctions now explored. First, the distinction between teleological and deontological moral theories will be clarified. This will be followed by developing the distinction between morality as "discovered" and morality as "invented."

Teleological Moral Theories

A teleological (Greek *telos*, for "aim" or "goal") view of morality holds that the moral goodness of an act depends on certain non-moral values (pleasure, peace, happiness) resulting from the act. For instance, utilitarianism maintains that an action may be certified as morally good if it produces a greater quantity of general happiness than unhappiness. From this perspective, you may be morally obligated to lie to an angry man waving a gun who has just asked you where your son could be found.

Deontological Moral Theories

In contrast, a typical deontological (Greek *deon*, for "duty" or "obligation") view of morality would hold that the moral quality of an act does not depend on its results but on some intrinsic value of the act itself. A deontological position may hold, for instance, that there is something morally wrong about telling a lie even if it would produce more general happiness than would truth-telling. Lying about your son's whereabouts to the angry man waving a gun would be morally wrong from this perspective. The moral philosophy of Immanuel Kant reflects such a deontological perspective. Most formulations of the "Divine Command" view in religious ethics would also reflect a deontological position in that this theory holds that an act X is morally right only insofar as God commands X, and an act Y is morally evil only insofar as God declares Y to be evil. An act is to be evaluated, not on the basis of its results, but on the basis of a Divine Command. X is right only because God declares that X is right.

Morality: Discovered or Invented?

Another significant distinction in moral philosophy can be made between those who hold that moral structures can be discovered in the very nature of things, and those who argue that moral structures or rules are human inventions designed to serve some human purpose. It is, of course, logically possible for one to actually invent ethical directives while believing that one has discovered them. Is the claim of knowing some divinely revealed moral truth, for instance, an invention of some kind or is it an actual discovery? The answer to such a question may necessarily be cast in terms of a certain faith judgment.

A THEORY ABOUT MORAL THEORIES

Morality Is Discovered

How, then, can morality be understood as an aspect of the very structure of reality, of the very nature of things? The most familiar view is presented in a variety of religious systems. Theists generally hold that the God who brought the world into being has also set forth a set of moral structures to be followed by morally responsible created creatures. The Ten Commandments, for instance, are believed by some theists to be revealed by God to Moses and represent an objectively true moral pathway that applies to all human beings. With these commandments comes the promise that those who obey will find themselves blessed in a variety of ways. On the other hand, Far Eastern religions—Hinduism, Jainism, and Buddhism—hold that certain basic moral realities are part of the very nature of reality and are expressed through the Law of Karma. Good deeds result in some form of reward for the faithful, and evil deeds bring about some forms of punishment, according to Karmic Law. But such Biblical laws or Laws of Karma are not seen by believers as inventions of human beings. These laws are, instead, part of the very structure of reality to be discovered, accepted, and obeyed.

Others have argued that morality is not to be discovered in some revealed divine law or Karma but through a rational analysis of human nature. If, for instance, human beings have an essential nature and if fulfillment or happiness is best achieved only through expressing that essential nature, then moral philosophy must consist in describing that essential human nature and showing how that nature can best be expressed or developed. Aristotle, for instance, held that human beings are essentially rational animals, and their happiness—the appropriate end for which they act—comes through the exercise of this rationality. Epicurus reflected a similar pattern of analysis in his egoistic hedonism whereby he claimed that right actions are those which maximize pleasure over pain for the one who so acts. This claim, too, was grounded in a belief about the essential nature of human beings. People, he taught, are strictly moral creatures with no meaningful existence beyond death and who appropriately and rationally seek to avoid pain and to experience pleasure during their limited years of life.

The Buddha—the "Enlightened One" (fifth to fourth century, BCE)—arrived at the Noble Truths through an analysis of our essential human condition. "To live is to suffer" was the first of his four noble truths. The remaining Noble Truths identified the cause of suffering and the remedy for it. The remedy—the noble eightfold path—involved a number of instructions. The point, here, is that neither Aristotle nor Epicurus nor the Buddha believed that they were *inventing* rules to help human beings through life. Instead, they believed they had discovered and described the essential nature of human beings. Furthermore, the point of the advice given by each was that of maximizing personal fulfillment for those who followed this advice. To be sure, their views of the nature of such fulfillment were strikingly different. In his quest for happiness, Aristotle's ideal man—and only a male can be such an ideal for Aristotle—has little resemblance to that of the Buddha's.

Another highly influential expression of the claim that morality is discovered, not invented, came from Immanuel Kant (1724–1804 CE) in his analysis of human reason. He shared with Aristotle and many others the assumption that our essential human nature is linked to the capacity to reason. In brief, Kant argued that reason was "given" to human beings so that they could be creatures with moral responsibility and a destiny. He believed that the features of a truly objective morality could be clarified by examining just how human beings do, in fact, think about matters moral. The conclusion of his argument led to his claim that a "categorical imperative" exists as the basic moral principle: "Act only on that maxim that you can, at the same time, will to be a universal law." Kant's subtle theory will be more fully developed in Chapter 3. In this context, his view is presented as another example of the claim that morality is an objective aspect of the nature of things and that the central truth of this morality can be discovered and clarified.

Morality Is Invented

On the other hand, a significant number of philosophers have defended the view that moral codes and moral theories are *invented*. Their claim is that morality is not some objective aspect of the way the world is constructed or the way in which human reason necessarily works. Rather, they believe that morality is a purely human invention designed to help people cope with the world as they experience it. Protagoras (490–420 BCE) may have been one of the earliest supporters of this position. He is famously noted for his claim that "Man is the measure of all things, of things that are, that they are, and of the things that are not, that they are not." In ethics, this claim led him to a form of ethical relativism in that he claimed there was no uniform moral law to be discovered that rightly pertains to human beings everywhere. Instead, each society or culture develops its own moral patterns and laws. He also asserted that there is no rational way to discern which of the varying rules and laws are right and which are wrong since no criteria exits, in principle, independent of particular cultures or societies. His advice, as a conservative, was to generally honor the patterns of one's own society since such rules are probably as good as any others. His analysis, critiqued by Plato, set the stage for arguments about ethical relativism all the way into the twenty-first century.

A more recent view of morality as "invented" was expressed by the French existentialist, Jean Paul Sartre (1905–80 CE). Having rejected both the existence of God and the view that there is some type of essential human nature to be expressed in life, Sartre concluded that there can be no objective way of validating moral choices. Yet life presses us into situations where we must make such choices. But in making these, he argued, we are condemned to be free. We must choose, but we have no way of rationally or objectively justifying or defending the morality of an action. According to Sartre, then, our own moral decisions derive entirely from our own subjectivity, which eliminates the possibility of any claim that we have somehow attained an objective moral truth.

The so-called emotive or "boo-hurrah" theory of ethics debated in the mid-twentieth century gave the entire argument about moral principles a radical reconstruction. Traditional moral philosophy generally considered moral judgments such as "killing innocent persons is wrong" to be either true or false. Hence, the task of the moral philosopher was that of showing how such judgments can be construed as true or false. The surprising claim of the emotivist view was that moral judgments are neither true nor false since they are merely *expressions* of emotions, not factual judgments of some kind. To assert that "killing is wrong," for instance, is the equivalent of uttering "boo to killing." Such "boo" utterances express emotions, but such expressions are neither true nor false. If someone says, "Boo to that team," it would not make sense to reply, "That's false" or "That's true." An appropriate response could be, "I feel different about that."

At this point I list the emotive theory among those that deny moral truths can be discovered in the nature of things since there are no such entities to be found. This would appear to leave the emotivist in the camp of those who hold that moral claims are invented since there are none to be discovered. Furthermore, for the emotivist, neither are there moral claims that can be invented. We are left, not with moral claims that can be true or false, but only with expressions that reflect our disapproval (boo) or approval (hurrah) of certain actions or states of affairs. Nevertheless, if our emotional responses are sufficiently strong, we may be prompted to take action regarding some event. David Hume's shadow lies behind this view of morality.

A Projection Theory of Ethics

The emotive theory of ethics suggests another theory that could explain how human beings invented ethics. Call it the "projection theory of ethics." Such a theory would grant that moral judgments are accompanied by certain emotional states. Thus, the judgment "That was an immoral deed" would be accompanied by a feeling of disapproval which could be expressed as "Phooey on that deed." Or, "That was a good deed" would be accompanied by a feeling of approval expressed as "Hurrah for that deed." But given that we experience these feelings of approval or disapproval, we then seek to invent ways to explain them or, more significantly, we invent ways of justifying the feelings we do have. (Therapists would grant that human beings have a great propensity for fabricating explanations that appear to justify their feelings or emotions.) And what could more adequately justify our feelings or approval or disapproval than the theory that such feelings are reflections of a basic moral order that exists in the universe?

Some cultural patterns and the myths that sustain them may reflect this kind of inventive rationalization. In traditional Hinduism, the feeling of superiority that the higher caste person has over the lower caste person—as well as the actions which flow from such caste structure—is neatly justified by the Law of Karma. "I am properly in this position of higher caste and you in the lower precisely because of the difference in the Karma which resulted, necessarily, from our deeds in our previous incarnation." Or, in the Biblical tradition, the first command given by God to the first man and woman could be seen as the attempt of the ancient Hebrews to give divine sanction to those activities they found to be central to their life experience. "Be fruitful and multiply, and fill the earth and subdue it, and have dominion over the fish of the sea and over the birds of the air and over every living thing that moves upon the earth" (Gen 1:28). The fruitfulness and dominion they experienced as factual become justified and explained as actions endorsed by God.

This projection theory of ethics may help explain how the very idea of moral rules came into being. Since I enjoy being treated in just and loving ways, justice and love must be fundamental principles built into the very nature of existence; therefore, God commands love and justice. And since I abhor theft and adultery, such actions must run counter to the fundamental nature of life and the commands of God. On the darker side, this theory may also explain why nations and cultures feel justified in wreaking havoc on enemies and neighbors—the cry of "God wills it" (*Deus volt*) in the Crusades, for example. How else do nations justify their prayers that God will help them crush the enemy?

I offer this short sketch of a projection theory of ethics as a tentative hypothesis. Even if true, the theory would not necessarily falsify any of the moral rules that may have arisen in this way. The origin of an idea does not necessarily justify or falsify the idea itself. The genetic fallacy identifies any such faulty inference. Furthermore, if this posited theory is true, it would be completely compatible with the major arguments put forward in this work. What I aim to show is that there are certain relationships between a moral system and the broader explanatory worldview in which the moral system is rooted. The connection could run in either direction. Given certain *beliefs* about the nature of things—a worldview—then some moral patterns appear to follow and would produce certain *feelings* about deeds deemed to be morally good or evil. Conversely, given certain *feelings* of compassion, sympathy, or anger, for example, we then invent *beliefs* about the nature of things—worldviews—that would justify the feelings we experience. While these connections appear to occur, they are not strictly logical connections.

While I have described the distinction between deontological and teleological theories of ethics in this chapter, I have not committed myself to either theory. And while I have suggested a number of ways in which morality can be viewed as discovered or invented, I have not committed myself to the truth of any such view of the origins of morality. As my argument moves forward, however, I must necessarily make some theoretical commitments of my own.

2

The Point of Morality

The concepts of moral and ethical arise because of conflicts of interest, and . . . moral systems have been designed to assist group members and explicitly not to assist the members of competing groups.

—R. D. Alexander[9]

Is it not significant that those who advocate self-sacrifice usually present it as a path to self-realization? "He who loseth his life shall find it." . . . If a man used moral language to commend not doing whatever would give rise to the flourishing of man as what he took man to be, then we should consider him irrational.

—W. D. Hudson[10]

ORDINARY LANGUAGE INVOLVES A variety of terms that usually reflect moral judgments of various kinds, such as "good," "bad," "right," "wrong," "ought," and "obligated." We are aware not only of those judgments but also of various laws, principles, and rules presumably employed in making them. Furthermore, we are familiar not only with the apparent authority these rules have in directing deliberate human actions but also with the many disagreements among people regarding those rules. As we live out our lives most of us operate with some semblance of a moral system that largely reflects the influence of those who nurtured us and helped shape our beliefs. We tend, intuitively, to trust these beliefs and call on them whenever we seriously engage in decisions about matters moral. Generally, we try to avoid being moral failures by our own standards.

Why Moral Systems and Codes?

The theory outlined in the previous chapter was formulated in order to explain certain phenomena related to the moral judgments people make. One basic phenomenon is that human societies appear, universally, to create moral systems and codes. What is there about our human situation that prompts us to develop such systems? Just what is the point of morality for human beings? What function does it have? These questions can be answered by constructing a series of scenarios, originally suggested by William James, which will help illuminate the point of morality by showing how experience forces human beings to make moral judgments.[11] The following exposition will draw heavily on certain moral intuitions that most of us hold but can serve to clarify the function of moral judgments.

Scenario I: A Non-sentient Universe

The first scenario presents a universe completely devoid of sentient creatures—those creatures or beings that have wants, needs, desires, pleasures, pains, or interests of any kind. Throughout this work, these "wants, needs, desires, etc.," will be referred to as WNDs. Such WNDs would include not only physical or bodily WNDs but also the entire potential range of human experiences—emotional, psychological, aesthetic, intellectual, social, spiritual, and mystical. Although this first scenario presents a universe devoid of human beings, animals, angels, and gods or *a* God, there could be a sun, stars, land, sea, clouds, and all related celestial and terrestrial phenomena. Even plants could be part of this universe if plants are not sentient beings.

Several observations can be made about this totally non-sentient universe. First, it would not contain any civil or statutory laws since such laws depend on a human or human-like agency to construct them. Next, this universe would be one devoid of *value*. In the absence of creatures that have WNDs, there would be no objects needed, desired, or valued. In order for something to *have* value, it must *be valued*. In this universe a rock might be broken or a tree shattered by a stroke of lightening, but these events would neither increase nor decrease value—assuming, again, that trees are non-sentient. An object could have *potential* value in the sense that it could potentially become the object of some sentient creature's valuing if such a sentient creature came into being. Finally, this proposed universe would also appear to be devoid of morality or of moral issues. Even if some *Karma* or moral law of cause and effect existed in this universe, such *Karma* would have no application since no actions having moral significance could take place.

Scenario II: One Sentient Being

A second scenario would be constructed by adding to the originally non-sentient universe one—but only one—sentient being that has WNDs. In this scenario, it is also assumed that no future potential sentient creatures would come into existence and that no gods or God exist. With the addition of that one sentient being, the universe would now include value since any object or state of affairs wanted, desired, or enjoyed by that creature would have value just because that creature valued it. What that single creature experienced as good *would* be a good. "Good" is used here in the non-moral sense, as we speak about a "good cake" or "good auto." What that creature experienced as "bad" would be bad in the non-moral sense.

This new universe would not yet include civil law. It would also be a universe without moral dimensions. The choices made by this one being could increase or decrease the amount of value experienced by that being, but the choices would have no moral implications. This creature could not be seen as *morally* bad. There would be no meaningful role for moral laws or moral decisions. This would be the case even if that one sentient being possessed those characteristics which are generally assumed to be necessary for moral capacities, such as freedom of action and the ability to understand the nature of moral obligation. In the absence of other human beings or sentient creatures, and if no future human beings or sentient creatures were to ever exist, a lone human being in that universe would have no moral obligations. Furthermore, that lone human being would appear to have no moral obligations toward herself. Her choices could produce increasing or decreasing satisfaction for her, but such choices would have no moral significance. Recall that no Divine Mind or Reality exists in this second scenario and that no future sentient beings will some day exist.

Scenario III: Two Sentient Beings

For the third scenario, add one more sentient being. Still neither god-like beings nor potential future sentient beings exist aside from the two introduced. There is a possible increase in value in this universe since there are two creatures that can value objects or states of affairs. This universe would also have the potential for morally significant actions. If these two creatures never interacted in any way, this universe would still be devoid of moral significance. Creature A could pursue its own goals without any concern for the impact on creature B's goals—and vice versa.

If, however, A's quest for its own perceived WNDs interacts or intersects with B's quest for its WNDs, then a new dimension has clearly appeared. Given such an interaction, a happy unity would exist if the WNDs of A were completely supportive and compatible with the WNDs of B—say, for instance, a truly perfect marriage in a truly perfect world. All the WNDs of both A and B could be honored, and no moral choices would need to be made. But if a clash of WNDs occurred with the interactions of A and B—if A desires to eat B and B desires not to be eaten by A—then the scene is radically altered. At this juncture some desires must be sacrificed if other desires are to be affirmed. There is a value conflict between these creatures. However, this setting may not yet have *moral* implications. Would a moral dimension exist if creature A were a human being and creature B a rabbit? Or what if creature A were a lion and creature B a human being?

Most readers would probably agree that a morally significant situation would exist in this third scenario if the two creatures were basically human in their makeup—that is, if both of them had the capacities and experiences which made it possible for them to think and act in moral terms and if some type of moral structures or laws existed. At this point, the question of what capacities and experiences are required for such thinking and acting is left open. Since no god-like being has been introduced into this universe, the question of just what kind of moral laws or codes could exist in this universe is also left open.

Given this third scenario, if the interests of two human-like beings are in competition, a number of questions arise that test our moral intuitions: How would such a clash of interests be arbitrated in that setting? If A felt threatened by or experienced a deep distaste for B, would it be *immoral* for A to take B's life? If so, why so? Or would it be *immoral* for B to enslave A if B found that to be both advantageous and possible? Again, if so, why so?

Our Moral Setting

This leads to the final scenario which shall be called "Our Moral Setting." This scenario is our present universe that is currently teeming with sentient creatures including some billions of human beings and possibly gods or a God. Occasionally, the WNDs of the sentient beings that exist in Our Moral Setting interact in positive and cooperative ways. At other times there are dramatic and bloody clashes of interest, as the struggles between certain species and the history of human warfare both bear witness. It is this final scenario that establishes the issues to be faced by any moral philosopher or system of ethics. Given Our Moral Setting, it is clear that not all the WNDs of all beings can be honored; indeed, some must be denied so that others can be affirmed. But how are these clashes of interest to be arbitrated? To reflect on morality is to come to terms with just such issues. In the end, the task of moral reflection is that of puzzling out how to appropriately arbitrate the many conflicts among the multitude of WNDs of various sentient beings existing in the world.

Given the scenarios examined, it seems intuitively clear that not all decisions or choices would constitute moral judgments. Whether I eat an apple or a pear would not appear to constitute a moral choice since it does not involved the WNDs of other sentient creatures. On the other hand, if I decide to eat well while fully aware that another human being with whom I could share such food is malnourished or starving, then it would appear that a moral situation is involved since there would be conflicting WNDs. In pursuing my desire to eat well, I am also frustrating the desire of those in need of food.

On Morally Significant Actions

If the interpretation of the scenarios described above is cogent, then any action that has moral significance will have at least six characteristics. 1) Such an action involves the WNDs of human beings and perhaps other sentient beings from animals to God or gods. 2) Such an action must in some way involve at least two sentient creatures with WNDs. A totally isolated creature cannot perform an action with moral significance. 3) Such an action requires a setting where there is a conflict between two or more sentient beings. Actions in an ideal world with no such conflicts would not have moral significance. An ideal world would, presumably, be one where the WNDs of various sentient creatures do not come into conflict and there are sufficient resources to meet all of the existing WNDs. 4) Such an action must be performed by a being with the capacity for making moral judgments. This being would be *aware* of the WNDs of other beings that are in conflict with its own (it recognizes a moral conflict). This being must *consciously* raise the issue of the proper prioritizing of the conflicting WNDs (It is aware of possible moral rules or principles). This being must be aware of the consequences of its actions regarding its own WNDs and those of competing creatures. Without such awareness, no actions would have moral significance though these could still be "good" or "bad" in a non-moral sense. A lion pursuing a gazelle seems not to be concerned about any moral issue at stake. Furthermore, we would also assume that no moral issue is, in fact, at stake in that encounter. Animals are not usually viewed as morally responsible creatures even though we reward and punish them for their behavior. We may refer to a dog as mean or nasty, but it would seem odd to speak of an "immoral" dog. 5) This being must be able to choose between various options while acting in this sphere of conflicting needs. This does not necessarily imply the need for freedom of the will, since the freedom to do what one wants can be seen as sufficient for moral responsibility. 6) Some type of action-guiding rules or principles or criteria must exist, though these could be either objective or subjective in nature. For instance, the very rational nature of persons may lead them to recognize a basic and objective moral principle (Kant). Or, the person may claim that his own needs have priority and that such subjectivity is an adequate defense of an action that is purely self-interested or self-referential (egoism). If the individual is not aware of any action-guiding principles, either objective or subjective, that person could not make a morally significant decision.

The Scope of Morality

This analysis of Our Moral Setting and its implications casts a wide net regarding morally significant actions. These actions would run far beyond lying, cheating, killing and adultery. If this analysis holds, then morally significant decisions abound in life. Choosing to spend money for costly vacations or meals instead of using it to help a child without nourishment or health care, would be making a morally significant decision since some WNDs are being satisfied while others are being "butchered," to use William James's term. In making such a choice, a person would presumably be willing to defend the choice by appealing to rules, principles, or arguments that would justify the choice. This analysis implies that the vast majority of civil laws and political decisions are morally significant since they almost always involved supporting the WNDs of some while sacrificing those of others. Laws against theft, for example, protect the WNDs of those who own food and frustrate the WNDs of others who could benefit by stealing food. (Was Robin Hood immoral?) The graduated income tax assumes that the wealthier members of society should be taxed so that services beneficial to others—such as free public education or universal health care—can be carried out. Political debate regarding such programs is grounded in a variety of assumed moral principles.

Alternative Views of Morality

Perhaps the analysis of the scenarios adapted from William James has led to a mistaken judgment about the nature of moral reality. Conceivably, moral judgments could be unrelated to the WNDs of sentient creatures. Perhaps moral reality is rooted in some aspect of the nature of things quite independent of such WNDs. Moral reality, for instance, may be based solely on the commands or laws of God that may have no relationship at all to the WNDs of created sentient beings. What that God commands will be morally right just because that God so commanded. Most religions, however, teach that God's commands are designed to help the believer flourish. Again, perhaps moral reality is grounded in the very nature of human rationality rather than in human WNDs, and these rational structures may at times be in opposition to the urgings of desires and wants. My major argument assumes that these alternative approaches to morality are mistaken in some way and that my original interpretation of the moral scene is more compelling.

In summary, my basic claim is this: *The point of the moral reflection that we necessarily pursue is to find appropriate ways of arbitrating among the various conflicting WNDs of sentient creatures*. Morality and moral reflection, when viewed in this manner, are necessarily part of human experience since we all must devise some method of arbitration that we deem appropriate. The meaning of "appropriate" is, of course, a crucial consideration in any moral theory and must be analyzed in the argument to be developed in this work.

In analyzing the point of morality and moral reflection, I did not attempt a *definition* of morality. Instead of giving a definition, I consider the point or function of morality. Two implications of this approach should be noted. First, any system of thought which seeks to find some means of arbitrating among conflicting WNDs would be classified as a moral theory. Thus, the egoistic hedonism of Epicurus will be understood to be a moral theory just as will Kant's formalism. Both Epicurus and Kant developed principles whereby persons could appropriately arbitrate among conflicting WNDs. Clearly, however, Kant's view of "appropriate" varied a good deal from that held by Epicurus.

A second implication of this approach is the rejection of the notion of "*the* moral point of view."[12] This phrase suggests that certain necessary conditions are involved in holding a *moral* point of view such that any theory lacking those conditions will fail to be a *moral* theory. Some conditions suggested by various philosophers include "impartiality" and "not being egoistic." Such conditions would rule out the hedonistic egoism of Epicurus as *a* moral point of view. In contrast, I suggest that Epicurus's theory should be considered a moral theory since his theory was also designed as a means of appropriately arbitrating among conflicting WNDs of sentient creatures. We may *reject* his moral theory but still accept it as a moral theory. My theory, then, constitutes a highly inclusive view of just what constitutes a moral theory. Again, the major aim of this work is to explain just *why* so many varying moral theories exist. In doing so, I neither support nor reject any traditional moral theory—religious or non-religious.

Conflicting *Personal* WNDs

Two major issues arise when seeking to appropriately arbitrate among competing WNDs. The first issue arises from the possible conflict among one's own WNDs. Which of my varied WNDs should I pursue through my actions? Which objects or states of affairs are most valuable to me? Not all of my WNDs can be honored. I cannot "have my cake and eat it too." The benefits of married life cannot be enjoyed while also enjoying the benefits of being single. Choices among my own competing WNDs will relate to my quest for a fulfilling life—as I understand what "fulfilling" might mean. Such a quest seems basically rational and has been supported by many significant philosophers including Plato, Aristotle, Thomas Aquinas, Spinoza, and J. S. Mill.

Yet the question of the fulfilling life which a rational creature would want to pursue is complex and linked to certain other questions about the nature of human beings. Six such questions are central: 1) Is there a meaning or point to the human venture? 2) Are we part of some Divine plan or are we the random products of an impersonal natural process? 3) How do human beings best find a sense of significance? We want not only to be but to be something of significance. This is deeply linked to a sense of dignity. 4) Is there a meaningful personal experience beyond the death of the body? If death is the end of the human venture, then it would appear that any fulfillment most come during bodily life. 5) Just what kinds of experiences lead to an individual's fulfillment? There are a variety of candidates: pleasure, tranquility, power, status. 6) Which human beings or other creatures contribute to my personal quest for fulfillment and which do not? In this quest, am I linked positively only to those within my clan, family, or tribe while other human beings are just "in my way"?

Moral Obligation

The second issue the moral philosopher must face while pursuing fulfillment is that of possible *obligations* to others as they seek their own fulfillment. In contrast to question 6, above, this issue carries with it the clear ring of moral language. To pursue what one believes to be fulfilling for oneself is to seek the "good life" in the usual non-moral sense of "good." In asking the question of possible obligation toward others, the question of the "good life" in the traditional *moral* sense of "good" is raised.

This second issue is also complex. Do we have moral responsibility toward all sentient creatures such that their quests for fulfillment have some claim upon our own lives? If so, why so? If not, why not? Or do we have moral responsibility only to other human beings? And, if not for all human beings, then which ones? Are there other powers or natural laws or gods or a God such that our WNDs and our quest for fulfillment are related in some meaningful way to the WNDs (commands, laws) of such powers? Do I honor such powers only insofar as they promise to benefit me as well; or must I honor their WNDs even when it involves a genuine cost to my own aspirations, goals, desires, and fulfillment?

Summary

In summary, I claim that the point of morality is to find a life pathway which leads to one's own personal fulfillment by pursuing those WNDs that promise to be most fulfilling. However, in the quest for my own fulfillment, I also must decide just how the WNDs of other sentient creatures relate positively or negatively to my own. Not all WNDs can be honored—my own or those of others. Some must be rejected if others are to come to fruition. The task, then, of moral reflection is to determine the most *appropriate* way to arbitrate among the competing WNDs. All fully developed moral theories address this task directly or indirectly. Chapter 4 will illustrate how this task is worked out in a number of classical and contemporary moral theories. Chapter 3 will examine varying views of the concept of "fulfillment" as it relates to broader worldviews.

3

Beyond Morality: Meaning and Significance

All religions are equally sublime to the ignorant, useful to the politician, and ridiculous to the philosopher.

—Lucretius (99–55 BCE)

Death . . . is nothing to us: when we exist, death is not present; and when death is present, we do not exist. Consequently it does not concern either the living or the dead, since for the living it is non-existent and the dead no longer exist.

—Epicurus (341–270 BCE)

For I am convinced that neither death, nor life, nor angels, nor rulers, nor things present, nor things to come, nor powers, nor height, nor depth, nor anything else in all creation, will be able to separate us from the love of God in Christ Jesus our Lord.

—Romans 8:38–39

Chapter 1 developed the claim that moral systems are attempts to find a fulfilling life pathway. Chapter 2 asserted that the point of the moral quest is to find some appropriate way to arbitrate among the competing wants, needs, and desires (WNDs) experienced by human beings and other sentient creatures. These two claims lead to at least two other questions: 1) In our quest for fulfillment, do we have any obligation to support other human beings and creatures in their quest for fulfillment? Chapters 6 and 7 explore this question. 2) What constitutes a truly fulfilling life, and how best to pursue that fulfillment? Chapter 4 will explore a variety of answers to this question in the context of various moral systems and their worldviews. Any fully developed moral philosophy must address both questions.

While the very idea of a fulfilled life is complex, philosophers have generally argued that rational persons seek such a life as they, themselves, understand "fulfillment." This chapter will examine the idea of a fulfilled life by analyzing two issues which make up the core of any concept of a fulfilled life. What is the *meaning* or point of our human life, if any? In the face of finitude and mortality, what basis is there for the *significance* of the individual person? While these two issues are often interrelated, they can be separated for our present purposes.

What Is the Meaning or Point of Human Life?

A person's quest for fulfillment necessarily hinges upon what they believe to be the point of the human venture from birth to death and perhaps beyond. Many of our day-to-day actions, and certainly our long-range plans and aspirations, will reflect our convictions about the meaning of our venture. The possible views held by human beings about the meaning of life are manifold, but most can be seen as variant forms of one of three basic views: nihilism, cosmic meaning, and temporal meaning.[13]

Before analyzing these alternatives, it would prove fruitful to explore just what we are asking about when we inquire about the meaning of life. Richard Taylor suggested that the question of life's meaning might best be explored by first constructing what might be thought of as a totally meaningless existence.[14] To do so, he analyzed the ancient Greek myth of Sisyphus. Sisyphus had angered the gods who then condemned him to the eternal labor of rolling a large boulder up a hill. However, each time he would almost reach the top of the hill, the rock would slip from his grip and roll to the bottom. He would then return to the bottom of the hill and begin, again, to roll the rock toward the summit—knowing full well he would never get it to the top. Taylor suggests this is a picture of an utterly meaningless existence. Like all great myths, of course, the story of Sisyphus is not just about some unfortunate figure who met a sad fate; it is, instead, the story of all human beings. Each day as we arise, we begin to roll some kind of rock, whatever our chosen ventures may be. And each day we retire, only to rise again the next day facing much the same activity. The Myth asks of us, "Toward what end or purpose do we live?"

Nihilism

There are voices who would answer that our fate, as that of Sisyphus, is a life without any meaning. Call these the Nihilists. Rejecting a religious interpretation of life, nihilism holds that just as there is no essential meaning or purpose to the universe, even so there is no essential purpose or meaning to human lives cast up randomly by this universe. Even our brief experiences of joy appear, upon reflection, to be empty. A striking literary expression of nihilism is found in Ernest Hemingway's short story, "A Clean Well-Lighted Place." The story explores the theme of nothingness as played out in the lives of various men spending an evening in a little diner. Near the end of the story, the main character utters a nihilistic revision of elements of Christian liturgy by substituting nada (nothing) for a number of key words in the Lord's Prayer and the Hail Mary.[15]

Cosmic pessimism—while not quite full nihilism—was expressed by Nobel-Prize-winning biochemist Jacque Monod:

> It is perfectly true that science attacks values. Not directly, since science is no judge of them, *and* must ignore them, but it subverts every one of the mythical or philosophical ontogenies upon which the animist tradition, from Australian aborigines to the dialectic materialists, has based morality, values, duties, rights, prohibitions.
>
> If he accepts this message in its full significance, man must at last wake out of his millenary dream and discover his total solitude, his fundamental isolation. He must realize that, like a gypsy, he lives on the boundary of an alien world; a world that is deaf to his music, and as indifferent to his hopes as it is to his sufferings or his crimes.[16]

While nihilism is a minority view, historically, nevertheless it is reflected by some voices in almost every age. The stories and traditions of various peoples and cultures serve as defensive counterpoints to the threat of nihilism.[17]

Cosmic Meaning

In sharp contrast to nihilism, cosmic meaning is rooted in some type of religious belief and thus is not an option for a worldview without some view of Divine or God. This view is most clearly expressed in—though not limited to—the theisms of Judaism, Christianity, and Islam in their traditional forms. Each of these would revise the Myth of Sisyphus by allowing him to live day by day while trusting that his life's venture will lead him to a joyous fulfillment after his death. En route, his rock rolling would include caring for his loved ones, his community, and humanity in ways revealed by the source book of his individual faith. Though his labors may be difficult, he is saved from emptiness and despair by his belief that the cosmos has meaning and purpose since it was brought into existence by God and will come to fulfillment under God's guidance. Human life, then, is part of that universe of meaning and believers trust that their lives are meaningful insofar as they participate positively in the work and will of God.

Cosmic meaning, like nihilism, can be reflected in art or literature. An example would be a prayer recited by a nurse at the close of the day to small orphaned boys in the film *The Cider House Rules*:

> O Lord, support us all the day long in this troublous life, until the shadows lengthen, and the evening comes, and the busy world is hushed, and the fever of life is over, and our work is done. Then of Thy mercy grant us a safe lodging and a holy rest, and peace at the last; through Jesus Christ our Lord. Amen.[18]

Temporal Meaning

The third major view of life's meaning can be called temporal meaning. This is essentially non-religious. While temporal meaning holds, like nihilism, that the universe has no essential meaning or point, nevertheless, human beings can find meaning in the joys and commitments they experience during their lifetime. Temporal meaning could be expressed in the Myth of Sisyphus if some alterations were made in the basic plot. For example, if Sisyphus managed to get his rock to the top and add even more rocks he could construct a home to provide shelter for himself and for those he loved. On the other hand, as Richard Taylor suggested, Sisyphus could find sufficient meaning if the gods injected a substance into his veins which would make him experience joy and satisfaction in the very rolling of the rock. The meaning would not be in the goal—since there is none—but in the journey.

It appears that this temporal meaning can be expressed in many ways. Some may find meaning exclusively in the pleasures they manage to experience; others may find meaning by devoting their energies to the service of others and the protection of planet earth's eco-system. The point here is that one's view of the meaning of life is crucially linked to what is deemed to be valuable and worth pursuing in the absence of religious consolations. Bertrand Russell once expressed a view of temporal meaning in vivid prose:

> Brief and powerless is man's life, on him and all his race the slow, sure doom falls, pitiless and dark. Blind to good and evil, reckless of destruction, omnipotent matter rolls on its relentless way; for man, condemned today to lose his dearest, tomorrow himself to pass through the gate of darkness, it remains only to cherish, ere yet the blow falls, the lofty thoughts that ennoble his little day; distaining the coward terrors of the slave of Fate, to worship at the shrine that his own hands have built, undismayed by the empire of chance, to preserve a mind free from the wanton tyranny that rules his outward life; proudly defiant of the irresistible forces that tolerate, for a moment, his knowledge and his condemnation, to sustain alone, a weary but unyielding Atlas, the world that his own ideals have fashioned despite the trampling march of unconscious power.[19]

Stages on Life's Way

Another analysis of the question of life's meaning was made by the Danish philosopher, Søren Kierkegaard, who sought to describe alternative attempts to make human life meaningful. He proposed that there are three "stages on life's way": the aesthetic, the ethical, and the religious. These stages do not necessarily represent a chronological sequence in a person's life, nor is it inevitable that a person will experience all three. According to Kierkegaard, an adult may choose to live in any one of the three, but since the stages are mutually exclusive, only one stage at any point in time. Furthermore, the choice is forced; a person must live either as an aesthete, or in the ethical stage, or in the religious stage. In selecting the stage, one selects the meaning of one's life.

The Aesthetic Stage

We must be content here with a brief description of Kierkegaard's stages, though such a description will not do justice to the subtle analyses he pursued.[20] Each stage is characterized by the way a person seeks to find meaning in life. In the aesthetic stage an individual finds meaning through the immediate experiences they find interesting and satisfying in some way.

Kierkegaard, no doubt, had in mind some of the Romantics of his day. Since such experiences constitute the meaning of life for the aesthete, the aesthete must, in principle, deny any constraints on the pursuit of such experiences. This implies the rejection of any moral rules that would inhibit or undercut the quest for such experiences. On the other hand, boredom is the great enemy of the aesthete since boredom is precisely the lack of immediate experiences which are interesting and satisfying. Curiously, boredom appears to be a problem only for the aesthete. Those in the ethical or the religious stage are seldom, if ever, bored.

The small child represents, for Kierkegaard, a paradigm case of the aesthete's quest for meaning. As long as the child is comfortable and has some interesting activity at hand, the child is generally happy—and life is experienced as meaningful. But if discomfort enters, or if the activity at hand no longer interests the child, then meaning is threatened and the child's world collapses. In a child this pattern is accepted as innocent and natural, but innocence disappears for the adult aesthete. The adult aesthete finds that they must constantly generate new activities or interests since most activities become dull upon repetition or as the aesthete matures. As an aesthete, the very small child is content for a few moments with toy blocks, but blocks seldom satisfy older children. They move on to other experiences—to the tricycle, then to the bicycle, then to the automobile. The present electronic age provides a vast array of interesting activities.

According to Kierkegaard's analyses, each step in this quest for experience has its moments of fascination and interest, yet each has some tendency to become dull and empty. Where does one go when the first car begins to lose its emotional luster? Perhaps a new model with more power or status would be of some interest. Then what follows? Kierkegaard suggests that aesthetes find themselves continuously threatened by the specter of boredom since they realize, perhaps only vaguely, that their quest for meaning is a sequence of experiences each of which tends to turn to emptiness and dust. Certain dimensions of the drug scene may be expressions of the aesthetic stage, though the motivation for drug usage may be that of escape from despair as often as it is a quest for a satisfying experience. The aesthete is continually threatened by the question, "Can this be all there is?" There is a constant need to push the experiential envelope.

Another paradigm for the aesthete, for Kierkegaard, is the legendary figure of Don Juan, who finds life meaningful through sexual encounters with a series of women. His attendant keeps a record of Dan Juan's ventures in various lands. However, as the legend suggests, this quest for meaning is ultimately undercut since meaning is rooted only in the vitality of the mortal body that eventually disintegrates. When the body fails, this quest for meaning fails.

While the child and the Don Juan figure exemplify the aesthetic stage of life, this stage can also be expressed in a variety of other ways that focus on meaning found through immediate experience. The intellectual aesthete finds meaning through the analysis and discussion of new ideas, new works of art and other creative activities. This stage can also be expressed in a religious mode when religious worship or participation is pursued purely as an experience of beauty or art or of "feeling good." To be sure, genuine worship no doubt can also *include* high experiences of beauty and art. Perhaps the aesthete of ordinary life finds life's central meaning searching the TV with a remote—or in going shopping. Jean-Baptiste Clamence, the central figure in Albert Camus's *The Fall*, is a striking literary representation of the collapse of someone in the aesthetic stage to a state of near despair.[21]

The Ethical Stage

If the aesthete is threatened by emptiness or despair, they may choose the ethical stage of existence where the core meaning of life is to be found in living out one's sense of moral duty as understood by the community. The person in the ethical stage does not reject pleasant experiences that life can bring—such as entertainment, good food, sexuality, and art—but the central meaning of life is not found in those experiences. Kierkegaard's paradigm for the moral life is the middle class "pillar of the community" of his Danish heritage. This person lives out their duties as parent, spouse, and contributing member of the community. These duties are pursued, not because they always bring satisfying and interesting experiences, but because of commitment to the responsibilities that have been assumed. The aesthete, on the other hand, would find that the satisfactions of marriage and family would eventually wear thin. If the aesthete tires of the duties linked to spouse and family, his remedy would be to withdraw from the commitments, trade in his wife for a new model—as he might his car—and live in a yacht off the coast of California, finances permitting.

The ethical stage does not necessarily imply a religious interpretation of life or of morality as an expression of God's will. Meaning, in this stage, is found in living by the socially established norms and rules of one's community. But the ethical stage of existence exacts its own costs, as Kierkegaard shows when he develops a type of Hegelian dialectic. The person who has chosen the ethical stage cannot, in principle, trivialize morality since the very meaning of life is at stake. The person, therefore, must take moral duty with deep seriousness. However, in doing so, can a man, for instance, be confident that he is the spouse, the parent, the worker, the neighbor, the responsible community member that he believes he should be? A serious commitment to moral duty can lay bare the inadequacy of his efforts and burden him with a feeling of failure and of guilt.

If the person who has chosen to live at the ethical stage of existence finds that their morality falls short of their aspirations, then the very meaning of life is threatened. Furthermore, they may come to feel imprisoned by a complex set of moral rules which were not of their making and which undercut any sense of individual personal identity. They find themselves to be merely a reflection of society's ideals and codes. Finally the specter of death begins to haunt. If life is one long attempt to live out difficult moral commitments, and all ends in death, perhaps one fares better by forgoing those commitments and returning to or adopting the aesthetic stage—which always stands as a possible option to be freely chosen. Again, despair looms on the horizon.

The Religious Stage

Given his passionate religious bent, Kierkegaard regards the religious stage as the only one that can ultimately rescue us from despair—the "sickness unto death." Persons who chose the religious stage are no ascetics. They do not forego life's rich experiences and the joys of embodied living, nor do they dismiss moral duty as a misguided concept. However, the meaning of life is now centered on the individual's relationship with God. All this is grounded in a faith that trusts beyond what can be known or verified through argument or evidence. This faith is a "leap" which is not achieved at one moment in life but by reaffirmation each day in the face of doubt and even anxiety. Faith does not overcome doubt since true faith is held only in the face of doubt. Faith is "treading water forty fathoms deep." The person in the religious stage realizes that faith is not a form of knowledge but is a chosen orientation which could, in principle, be mistaken.

Kierkegaard maintains that the bartender at the local pub may be existing in the religious stage while the clergyman may not be. This is very possible since faith is an intensely interior reality and does not necessarily show itself in outward demeanor or in babbling about matters explicitly religious. In the religious stage, the person finds that the anxiety of guilt is muted since they find themselves to be accepted, forgiven, even though they fail at times to be what they are called to be or desire to be. Also, in that stage, the anxiety of death is overcome in the trust that one is secured by the Infinite, both now and beyond death. Finally, in the religious stage the anxiety of emptiness and meaninglessness is overcome. Meaning is now rooted in the Eternal, not the ephemeral.

Empirical Research on Meaning of Life

Up to this point the analysis of the meaning of life has been largely philosophical in nature. There is empirical research that addresses this issue and links it to other dimensions of human experience. Scholars interested in the psychology of religion have developed instruments that attempt to measure whether an individual's level of life's meaning is high or low.[22] Research tends to show that a person with a high sense of meaning has relatively clear goals, sees reasons for existence, sees himself or herself as responsible, is prepared to die, and perceives life as a mission. Those with a low sense of meaning have opposite characteristics and are described as reflecting an existential vacuum or frustrated will to meaning.

Other researchers have developed instruments designed to detect the values that people tend to pursue in life. In his "Value Survey," Milton Rokeach listed eighteen "terminal values"—end states pursued—which include the following: a comfortable life, an exciting life, pleasure, a sense of accomplishment, family, security, mature love, salvation, and self-respect. Subjects who took this value survey were asked to rank the eighteen items in order, listing their highest value as number one. Given this research, psychologists began to ask if there were any correlation between the meaning of life indicated with the values preferred. They discovered that only four of the terminal values had any significant relationship to the level of meaning which persons expressed: pleasure, excitement, comfort, and salvation. Of those four values, only salvation was positively related to a sense of purpose or a meaning in life. Those who ranked salvation as a high value tended to have a higher score on a Purpose-in-Life Test. On the other hand, subjects who ranked pleasure, excitement, and comfort high on their values list tended to have low purpose-in-life scores, and those who ranked those three values low tended to have higher purpose-in-life scores.

While this data shows some interesting correlation between what is valued and the meaning of life, it in no way proves that some values or meanings are "better" than others. Such science helps to show what *is* the case, but cannot show us what *ought* to be the case. Those familiar with sociologist Peter Berger's *The Sacred Canopy: Elements of a Sociological Theory of Religion* would probably expect to find a correlation between "salvation" and a high sense of meaning in life. Berger and other sociologists consistently claim that one of the major *functions* of religion is just that of helping to supply such meaning. These sociologists would note, however, that even if religion does tend to supply meaning to life, such a fact does not imply that religious belief, as such, is true. Furthermore, a correlation between goals such as pleasure, excitement, and comfort with a low sense of life's meaning—a tendency toward despair—would have been fully anticipated by Søren Kierkegaard. Such values would be closely related to the values pursued in the aesthetic stage of life as Kierkegaard described it.

Significance in the Face of Finitude and Mortality

Human beings not only want to *be*, they want to be *significant*. They want to *count* in some way. Ernest Becker shaped this issue clearly when he observed

> What man really fears is not so much extinction, but extinction with insignificance. Man wants to know that his life has somehow counted, if not for himself, then at least in a larger scheme of things, that it has left a trace, a trace that has meaning.[23]

This individual quest for significance is an intimate aspect of the search for fulfillment. The sense of individual significance, however, can be undercut by a variety of circumstances. Unsatisfactory personal relationships can weaken our sense of significance if those who should love us and support us fail in some basic way to do so. Perceived inadequacies and limitations of various kinds—physical attributes, intellectual capacities, even social and creative skills—can threaten our sense of significance.

Many observers of the human scene note that a sense of cosmic insignificance can also threaten us. Pascal once expressed this anxiety:

> When I consider the brief span of my life, absorbed into the eternity before and after, the small space I occupy and which I see swallowed up in the infinite immensity of space of which I know nothing and which knows nothing of me, I take fright and am amazed to see myself here rather than there; there is no reason for me to be here rather than there, now rather than then. . . . The eternal silence of these infinite spaces terrifies me.[24]

The character of Calvin, a small precocious child in the comic strip Calvin and Hobbes, often expressed much the same mood in contemporary and popular terms. Standing alone under the great dome of a starry sky or in the face of the awesome power of nature, Calvin insists that he is significant. Nevertheless, in spite of his protestations of significance, he quietly concludes that he is hardly more than a dust speck.

Existentialist philosophers, theologians, and psychologists have suggested that existential anxieties about death and meaninglessness represent threats to our sense of significance. According to Paul Tillich, these anxieties are "existential" in the sense that they are inherently part of the human experience and must be borne.[25] While drugs and alcohol may deaden our sense of these anxieties, and sexual ecstasy and shopping may distract us momentarily, neither psychiatry nor religion can remove these anxieties. They must be borne through the "courage to be." Indeed, one of the major functions of religious belief is that of supplying a "sacred canopy" under which the believer lives and which provides a basis for such courage. This sacred canopy, however, does not remove the anxieties; at best it helps to undergird the courage needed to bear them.

Death Anxiety

Anxiety about death may be primary. Ernest Becker argued,

> the idea of death, the fear of it, haunts the human animal like nothing else; it is a mainspring of human activity—activity designed largely to avoid the fatality of death, to overcome it by denying in some way that it is the final destiny for man.[26]

Plato observed, "the one aim of those who practice philosophy in the proper way is to practice for death and dying."[27] According to the Buddhist tradition, the one who became the Buddha was compelled to pursue his quest for enlightenment because of the "four passing sights" which included disease, old age, and death.[28] And Saint Paul, writing to the Corinthians, refers to death as the "last enemy to be destroyed."[29] More recently, Sigmund Freud reflects on the "painful riddle of death" and "the great necessities of fate against which there is no remedy."[30]

While all animals die, it appears that human beings are unique in that they come to *know* that they must die. Thus, for human beings, death brings with it certain conceptual problems that other creatures need not face, for we must somehow integrate this consciousness of our mortality into the cluster of beliefs which make up our worldview. The idea of death is, when examined, quite complex. Children come to the "adult" view of death in three identifiable and discreet stages: 1) that the body ceases to function, 2) the person who died will not return, and 3) *all* persons someday die. The third level of understanding is usually in place when the child is some ten years of age. Small wonder, then, that religious traditions begin to bring in religious rites and intellectual defenses against the threat of death in the early years of the second decade.

Defenses Against the Threat of Death

A major human strategy used in defense against personal mortality is to construct some view which helps the person deny that death has the last word. These views can be identified into various schemes of immortality. Some philosophical positions, such as Plato's, put forward the claim that the human soul is immortal and survives the death of the physical body which, in life, is the "prison house of the soul." The Biblical traditions—Judaism, Christianity, and Islam—speak not so much of the immortality of the soul as they do of the "resurrection of the body," thus giving the body an affirmation which Plato refused to do. The religious traditions of India have generally muted the sting of death by postulating the theory of reincarnation or transmigration of the soul. However, in that tradition, the very thought of the continuous reincarnation was rejected as unbearable; hence the ultimate goal is that of absorption into the Divine sea of reality—union with Brahman.

Naturalistic thinkers who reject the idea of personal immortality or the resurrection of the body have come to terms with their mortality in a variety of ways. Epicurus, the ancient Greek atomist and hedonist, held that death can be explained as the coming apart of the "atoms" which make up all existing things. Since a person is nothing more than a functioning collection of material atoms, at death the person essentially ceases to be. Such an understanding of death has its comforts since it implies that after death there is no suffering to be anticipated, and the gods cannot punish us in an afterlife since we are no more. During our living years, then, Epicurus taught that we should live a life of pleasure for the self with "pleasure" defined as "absence of pain in body or mind." Our concern for others, he taught, was to be limited to those actions which redound to our own benefit.[31]

Symbolic Immortality

Other naturalist philosophers have suggested various forms of symbolic immortality which function as ways of stripping death of its capacity to annihilate the individual. While these thinkers grant that their own existence as a conscious entity is no longer possible after death, they take some consolation in knowing that their existence will have an influence on future events and future beings in a number of ways. Thus, the biological mode of symbolic immortality is that of living on through one's children, while to the socio-biologist mode, one lives on in the tribe or clan or nation with which one identifies. Another position suggests that a creative person can live on, symbolically, by way of great works of art or heroic deeds. For example, Shakespeare, Tolstoy, Rembrandt, Newton, and Einstein are able to "live on" through their works. Persons with a deep sense of identity with nature and its vitalities can find a form of symbolic immortality in the understanding that their bodies return to the earth and join in the great creative processes of nature.

Psychiatrist Robert Lifton suggests there are those who find no effective shield from their finitude in either the actual or symbolic forms of immortality.[32] These persons may express what he calls "experiential transcendence" as a means of blunting their sense of transience. This transcendence may be found in intense feeling states which cover anxieties and represent forms of denial. Thus, in various forms of ecstasy and rapture, one seeks to live only in the intense experiences of the moment or else seeks a state of numbness or insensitivity with the help of various chemicals. Lifton's "experiential transcendence" is a modern formulation of Kierkegaard's aesthetic stage of existence.

Anxiety of Meaninglessness

While anxiety about death may be the most basic of existential anxieties, meaninglessness can also undercut attempts to find a fulfilled life. A common epitaph on grave markers in the ancient world expressed this sense of meaninglessness: *Non fui. Fui. Non sum. Non Curo.* (I was not. I was. I am not. I do not care.) Poets have voiced this anxiety with great clarity, as Lucretius in his "On the Nature of Things," to Shelley's "Ozymandias," and Mathew Arnold's "Dover Beach." While such anxiety has often been expressed in cultures, it is usually muffled by cultural meaning systems, often religious in nature. When these systems of meaning are secure, the anxiety of meaninglessness rarely comes to the conscious level. Successful cultures tend to provide meaning systems which give support to the vast majority of citizens through explanations of "why things are the way they are." The Brahmin in traditional India felt secure in his high-ranking caste, while the person in the lower caste accepted their situation as the appropriate working out of the cosmic Law of Karma. Plato, in his ancient Greek setting, opined that every culture needs some kind of story or myth to the effect that some persons are made of gold, while others are made of silver, bronze, iron, or clay. Only then will the persons in the lower rank find their position acceptable. When these established systems of cultural meaning begin to dissolve, transformations take place, and the problem of meaninglessness begins to surface.[33] Historic transformations often lead to the establishment of new cultural meaning systems.

Religious Means of Significance

Human ingenuity may be most strikingly demonstrated by the modes in which persons seek to invent or establish personal significance in the teeth of death and possible meaninglessness. While religious traditions often emphasize human frailty and brokenness—"Thou art dust, and to dust thou shalt return" (Gen 3:19)—they ultimately seek to provide a grounding of our significance in some eternal dimension. If a religion cannot deal successfully with the basic anxiety of personal insignificance, that religion will never develop or sustain a following. Christianity appears to hold the most pessimistic view of human nature and the human condition since Original Sin places everyone in a state of alienation from God even at birth. While deepening the human problem, Christianity exalts the gracious nature of God. A crucified Messiah presents a radical solution to a radical problem. Ultimately, the freely given grace of God overcomes the alienation and brings the individual back into eternal reconciliation with the Divine. Significance is found in being loved and redeemed by God's own self-giving. This theology reflects the dynamics of "truth and reconciliation" movements.

Hinduism provides the most expansive basis for significance by identifying our true self with Brahman, the Ultimate Reality: *Tat twan asi.* "That art thou." Individual selfhood is an illusion; the true self is identical with the Divine. Other religious traditions assure their followers that they are among the chosen or the elect, or that every individual soul is created, sustained, and loved by the Infinite. Buddhism's approach to individual significance is, at first blush, paradoxical.[34] The Buddha taught the "no self" doctrine as part of the answer to the suffering that human life confronts. We are not abiding selves, souls, or spirits, rather we are a process that moves from moment to moment with no abiding self "behind the scene" having the experiences. We are the experiences. But with the realization of the no-self, we can find the detachment from the world where "ignorant craving" brings suffering.

Historically, religions have tended to provide the worldviews that inform most cultures. But with the erosion of religious worldviews, cultures have become replete with many secular symbols of significance: wealth, power, community status, intelligence, popularity, creativity, beauty, or strength. Contemporary advertisements suggest that we gain significance insofar as we wear the right clothes, drive the right car, live in the right part of town in the right kind of house with the right kind of furnishings, engage in the right kind of activities, and belong to the right class or group of people. The psychologists designing such advertising assume to know where our personal significance buttons are located and how they can be pushed.

Secular Significance

On the other hand, a secular point of view can also yield a sense of significance by way of creative contributions to the human community through art, science, industrial production, invention, and perhaps even philosophy. Humanists find significance in their commitments to the well-being of the human community and the creative labors which sustain and enrich cultures. Some secularists can also find significance by identifying with nature and preserving the environmental processes which nourish the rich variety of life forms.

Human history can perhaps be most clearly understood as the history of creatures that are conscious of their mortality and seek to wring some mark of significance and meaning from the world. In this sense, every person wants to be a "hero" of some kind—if not the high heroism of generals and kings, at least as counting for something in one's own family or community. Ernest Becker observed, "The question that becomes then the most important one that man can put to himself is simply this: how conscious is he of what he is doing to earn the feeling of heroism."[35]

This chapter has been purely descriptive in its aim to portray how human beings have sought after a fulfilling life which would include some sense of meaning and significance. Contrasting world views, naturalistic or theistic, tend to reflect contrasting visions about this quest. The question of which scheme of things is most appropriate is left open. Our personal journey for a fulfilled life leads us necessarily to personal commitments on specific issues and broader worldviews.

4

Moral Theories and Worldviews

Without religion there can be no real, sincere morality, just as without roots there can be no real flower.

—Leo Tolstoy[36]

We have been so conditioned and enervated by the Beatitudes that we are hardly capable any longer even of understanding . . . the truth that was so obvious to the pagan moralists: that what is worth having is not the common, but the uncommonly good.

—Richard Taylor[37]

Two claims about any complete moral theory are central to this work. First, such a theory must provide an answer to the question of what type of life is most fulfilling for a human being—the question of the fulfilled life. Second, it must also show what obligations, if any, a person has to help others who also seek a fulfilling life—the question of moral responsibility. In this chapter a number of influential moral theories will be reviewed showing how each theory answers these questions from within the context of the philosopher's worldview.[38] The list of theories is by no means comprehensive. I have selected only a few to serve as examples that illustrate a major theme of this work. These overviews will not attempt to provide comprehensive descriptions of the philosophy or moral theory of these philosophers. Standard works should be consulted for more detailed and nuanced interpretations. Instead, these overviews are intended to demonstrate that beliefs about the fundamental nature of reality—some form of the divine or naturalism—shape answers to the two questions above. My aim is to be purely descriptive; no attempt will be made to evaluate the views presented. While religious systems of the Far East could be included in this overview, I narrow the discussion to Western worldviews for simplicity and illustration.

Epicurus (341–271 BCE)

Stepping out of strict chronological order, Epicurus is presented first to model a theory that clearly reflects the themes in this work. This Greek philosopher developed perhaps the clearest moral theory ever formulated.

Furthermore, Epicurus has had a following throughout history as well as in the modern world. The moral pathway he describes follows directly from the views he held about the fundamental nature of reality and human nature.

His worldview was influenced by earlier Greek philosophers who had criticized the standard myths of Greece and developed natural explanations of the world of experience. They sought to understand nature (Greek *physis*) by way of observation and reasoning and thereby helped to pave the way for the pursuit of physics, chemistry, biology, and astronomy.

Greek Atomists

Epicurus adopted the views of earlier Greek philosophers who held that everything in the universe is made up of small uncreated, eternal, and unbreakable units of matter they called atoms. ("Atom" in Greek means "uncuttable.") These units of matter are arranged in space in a variety of ways that result in such things as trees, clouds, and human beings. This atomism is an early form of ontological materialism and formed the basis for the worldview expressed by Epicurus. According to this theory, the entire universe is an expression of eternally existing and uncreated atoms with no divine hand or mind guiding the process. Human life, therefore, is the product of these purely natural processes which have no purpose, goal, or point.[39]

Epicurus's worldview was essentially naturalistic. He granted that gods might exist, but it they do, they also exist as some combination of atoms. Even if they did exist, they would be of no concern for human beings since they had no way of intervening into human affairs. Furthermore, these gods were of no threat to human beings after death since human beings cease to exist after death. Human beings do not *have* bodies; they *are* bodies. After the body dies, the atoms go about other activities. There is no such thing as a soul or mind that exists beyond the death of the body. These views, Epicurus would add, help us to avoid fear of the gods since these gods cannot intervene in our earthly life and cannot harm us after death since we no longer exist after the death of the body. This view led to the Epicurean epitaph: *Non fui, fui, non-sum, non-curo* ("I was not; I was; I am not; I do not care").

Egoistic Hedonism

The moral theory proposed by Epicurus was an early form of egoistic hedonism, which asserts that the good and fulfilling life is made up of pleasure for the self. In this teaching he accepted what all major moral theories assume—that the aim of a rational and morally appropriate life is that of personal fulfillment. He did not deny the possibility of purely altruistic deeds, but he would consider them to be irrational. Others should pursue pleasure for themselves as they see fit. This view of morality seems to flow directly from his worldview. If there is no aim or point to the universe, and if we live a limited number of years as a cluster of atoms, and if we have no personal existence after death, then it follows that the rational human being would seek a life of pleasure and try to avoid pain during mortal life. Avoidance of pain seemed primary, for Epicurus, since he defined "pleasure" as the "absence of pain."

A rational person is also a prudent person, according to Epicurus. The rational person must consider the help or harm that might ensue from relationships with others. In giving help to others, the proper motive would be that of seeking pleasure for oneself. Beyond this motive there is no obligation to be of aid to others. He cautioned against marriage, not because sexuality, as such, was evil, but because marriage usually involves love for the spouse and for the children born of the union. However, mates and children die, and this death brings much pain. Thus better to never love at all than to love and to lose. The best of times would be that of a gathering of good friends talking philosophy and sharing good food and wine. He cautioned against wild parties since these tended to result in pain the next day. He was known to be a warm friend, a gracious host, and a pleasant companion.

Epicureanism as a Moral Theory?

Some would argue, as we shall see in chapter 7, that egoistic hedonism is not a moral theory since it runs counter to the main strands of morality in most cultures. Some might claim, for instance, that any moral rule should apply universally to everyone. However, they would continue, the rule to maximize one's own self-interests could not be universalized by an Egoist. If I, as an Egoist, tell others to maximize their self-interest, that would seem to run afoul of my own interests. An Egoist, therefore, would prefer that others should *not* seek to maximize only their own interests. It does seem possible that Epicurus, himself, would reject that argument. He did, after all, advise others to maximize their self-interests as rational persons. No doubt his friends knew of this advice and may well have followed it. Epicurus leaves us with the advice of prudence. In rationally seeking our own interests, we must be aware of how this seeking impinges on the lives and interests of others. The best policy would appear to be that of *reciprocal altruism* whereby prudential actions help the egoist to maximize their self-interests. Such reciprocal altruism as practical advice does not contradict the Egoist's central motive. The happiness of others can contribute to our own happiness. The advice that everyone should maximize their self-interest is not self-contradictory; it merely recognizes the reality of the human situation as Epicurus viewed it. Epicurus certainly did not advise that we should love our neighbor as ourselves.

I include Epicurus in the list of theories about morality for a number of reasons. His theory is, after all, discussed—often critically—in most standard histories of ethics.[40] Furthermore, his theory does address the major task of any moral theory: how best to arbitrate among the competing wants, needs, and desires of sentient creatures. His theory also addresses the two major issues in moral theory which I have proposed: first, he proposes a pathway that will lead to a fulfilling human life—pleasure for the self; then he addresses the question of obligation toward others by asserting that we have no obligation to aid others except insofar as any aid we offer to others redounds to our own pleasures. His moral theory has a certain familiar tune as we reflect on the apparent goals often hyped in our culture. Epicureanism remains, for some, a viable moral theory within the context of a naturalistic worldview.

Charvaka of India

The Epicurean worldview and moral theory is not limited to Western cultures. A parallel is found in Charvaka, a philosophical system in ancient India that rejected the classical scriptures of India such as the Vedas and the Upanishads. Charvaka taught that there is no meaningful divine or spiritual reality and that all existing things are products of material processes which operate, without goal or intent, on the basis of their own laws. The system held that human beings, like other creatures, are products of the mindless processes of matter. Death ends the existence of the individual human being. During life, therefore, the rational person seeks to avoid pain and to gain pleasure. We live prudently with others, but we have no obligation to aid them. Both Charvaka and Epicureanism have been minority positions in their cultural traditions. Nevertheless, both represent positions that have attracted, intrigued, and annoyed many who have pondered the human venture.

Plato (430–347 BCE)

Often cited as the father of Western philosophy, Plato left an enormous imprint on thought and culture. This chapter will lift out only the aspects of his thought which illustrate how his worldview shaped his claims about what constitutes true human fulfillment and the nature of moral obligations to others. Standard sources should be consulted for a complete exposition of Plato's thought.

Challenges Plato Faced

Plato set his mind to the task of overcoming challenges that had arisen in the Greek culture of his day. A number of philosophers had rejected the mythical traditions that had served both as religion and as science. In doing this, some thinkers rejected the idea of God or gods and sought to explain the world in purely natural terms. Another challenge came from those who tended to undermine the basis for morality by claiming that talk about morality and justice was just a matter of high-sounding words and had no grounding in reason. Morality and law were merely human constructs. They were invented by human beings and could be changed by human beings. Genuine knowledge about morality and justice was not possible.

Plato also faced the universal challenge to all human beings—the problems of finitude and death. These problems bring with them the very question of the meaning or point of the human venture. In his ambitious undertakings, Plato sought to develop a political, social, and moral philosophy while also laying a foundation for genuine knowledge and a solution for the problem of death.

Plato on "God"

Plato rejected the view of the gods in traditional Greek mythology as totally inadequate. He did not, however, appeal to some revealed truth in formulating his own view of God. For Plato, belief in God had to be on the basis of careful reasoning. The views he developed about God and the gods have little resemblance to the God of Western theism, although these later theisms reflect traces of Plato's philosophy. In his late dialogue, *Laws*, he developed the first attempts in Western philosophy at proofs for the existence of God. In that dialogue, Plato sought to prove that gods do exist, that they care about human beings and their behavior, and that these gods cannot be flattered or bribed to benefit an individual.

World's Origin: "A Likely Story"

An approach to understanding Plato's belief about God (or the gods) might best begin with Plato's account of the formation of the world. Plato developed what he called "a likely story" to put forward his theory. He acknowledged that the task was ambitious, but he held that his view was a rationally compelling one. Our universe, so Plato taught, came about by way of an interaction of three eternal and uncreated factors or entities: 1) pre-existing chaotic matter; 2) a Demiurge (Craftsman) or God; 3) a realm of "Forms" (ideas) that functioned as patterns for the Craftsman. The world as we know it was brought into being, according to this story, when the Divine Craftsman used the Forms as pattern to put the chaotic matter into order. Every existing material entity was made on the basis of some such Form. What we experience as a tree, for instance, is an entity resulting from the basic matter being shaped into the Form or pattern of "treeness." This theory also accounts for cats, salamanders, and human beings. We moderns might think of this theory as an early attempt at envisioning DNA.

Plato's God, being good himself, desired to reflect his own perfection in something outside of himself; therefore, he used the realm of unchanging forms to fashion the changing world of sense experience as far as this was possible. However, the chaotic matter used by this God was stubborn and could not be formed into a perfect world. In this story, Plato absolves this God of any responsibilities for the faults that may occur in this world. The imperfections, sufferings, and evil that arise in the world are laid at the door of this stubborn matter, not the Craftsman.

Origin of Human Souls

Plato's likely story also accounts for human souls and helps establish the major factors in Plato's moral theory. In addition to fabricating the material world, Plato's God also created a world soul and the heavenly race of the gods. The race of the gods appears to be gods of the fixed stars and planets. These gods exist in order to carry out the will of the Divine Craftsman. The gods serve God. Parallels to the idea of angels in Western monotheism seem clear. In all of this Plato insists that Mind or Reason is the ultimate ground of purpose and direction. Plato's view could be seen as an early formulation of the idea of laws of nature, both in the moral and scientific sense. For Plato, the world is not to be seen as the product of randomness and chance.

Plato's account of the origins of human souls involves mythological language. Rational human souls were created by the Divine Craftsman (God) and inhabited a star at one time. Some of these souls developed a desire for the world of sensory experience and became enclosed in a material body. This body is a "prison house" for the soul. Plato indulges in a Greek pun in this account using "*soma*" (body) and "*sema*" (prison). Before its "fall" into a material body, the soul had direct knowledge of the Forms. When entering the body, however, the rational aspect of the soul becomes confused by the addition of desiring and spirited dimensions of the soul as well as by sensory experience. These souls, however, may free themselves from their material prison and return to their star by overcoming the lower aspects of the soul through the use of reason. If the soul fails in this endeavor, it can sink to lower levels and enter a series of animal bodies as stages in the process of purification. This view is similar to the doctrine of the transmigration of souls expressed in India. This dualism between spirit (good) and matter (evil) still haunts Western thought.

Elements of the Human Soul

Plato develops a theory about the human soul as he analyzes the nature of a person who is just or good. The Greek concept of "soul" (psyche) was used to explain just why some things have life and some do not. Rocks do not have life; but plants, animals, and human beings do have life. Thus "psyche" names a life principle that accounts for the presence of life. The human soul, as Plato explains, is made up of three distinct parts—the "desiring," the "spirited," and the "rational"—each with its appropriate function or role. The desiring aspect relates to appetites for food, drink, and sexual satisfaction. The spirited aspect involves such things as strength of will, anger, shame, and conscience. While animals have the desiring and spirited aspects of soul, they do not have the rational aspect. Here the Greeks shared the almost universal human conviction that human beings differ from animals in highly significant ways.

Reason, for Plato, is that aspect of the soul that should rule and direct the other two. In one image, he suggests that reason is like a charioteer guiding the chariot of life which is pulled by two horses—a wild and unruly horse (desiring) and an energetic but more disciplined horse (spirited). A life is well lived when reason controls the other elements of the soul. When reason controls, there is harmony in the soul, and the person is a just person. If reason fails in its role to direct a person's life, that person is dragged down by the drives of the desiring element of the soul and leads to a less satisfactory life. This analysis is akin to the Buddha's assertion that suffering (*dukkha*) is the result of ignorant craving (*tanha*).

Yearning for Immortality

There is in Plato the man, as well as in his thought, a deep yearning for some type of existence beyond the transient, changing, and misleading world of sensory experience. He accounts for this yearning with his doctrine of *eros*. The experience of beauty in the sensory world inspires in the soul a yearning for the ideal Form of beauty which the soul contemplated in its previous existence among the stars. It is this yearning which leads to the craving for fame, the urge to create art, science, and philosophy. It also expresses the longing for immortality. Plato suggests, here, that fame and creativity are forms of *symbolic* immortality since the person lives on by way of their fame or creations. Children have a similar function. The yearning for personal immortality, however, is central.

Plato develops a curious argument in support of the immortality of the soul. Since this longing for immortality is part of our essential nature, Plato posits that the fulfillment of that longing must be possible. It is as though this natural longing of the soul must be honored in a good universe. Any such deep natural longing that would be, in principle, impossible to fulfill would reveal a deep flaw in the created nature of things and would call into question the goodness of the Divine Craftsman.

Morality: The Good Life

Plato reflects the common belief that morality is advantageous—that the good life in the moral sense is also the good life in the non-moral sense. For Plato, the just person is the happiest person. He held to a form of psychological egoism in asserting that persons want individual happiness and that any action is chosen because that person believes the action will bring about personal well-being. The problem, Plato recognized, is that while the quest for happiness is normal and legitimate, beliefs about just how to achieve such happiness are often mistaken.

Herein we find the significance of the role of reason in developing the art of living. For Plato, this art of living requires an understanding of the role of the three parts of the soul. Each part has its corresponding virtue when under the direction of reason. Temperance is the virtue related to the desiring element of the soul; courage is the virtue related to the spirited element; and wisdom is the virtue related to the rational aspect of the soul. When reason properly rules, then the fourth virtue—justice—is achieved by way of the harmony of temperance, courage, and wisdom.

A life which has achieved this harmony would reflect the generally accepted values of community life in Plato's day—truthfulness, honesty, loyalty to one's family, friends, and community. However, Plato asserts that these practices do not make the person good. Rather, the person who has become good by way of reason will live out such practices. Martin Luther, the sixteenth-century Reformer, expressed much the same position in holding that good deeds do not make the good man, but a good man does good deeds.

God and Morality

In his latest and longest dialogue, *Laws*, Plato develops his views about the significance of God in matters moral. The dialogue takes place among three older men who are attempting to outline a constitution for a new city. This work—often highly criticized—was the product of his later years and probably reflects a more conservative turn in his thinking. He maintains that God (gods) has an important role in morality by dealing with human beings through a system of rewards and punishments. These sanctions can extend to life after the death of the body and determine the destiny of the soul.

The aim of this moral system, Plato posits, is to maximize the goodness of the world. While God cares for the individual as part of the whole and for the sake of the whole, Plato does not believe that God loves us as individuals. Neither should human beings love God or the gods. Instead, the gods serve as models to be imitated since they are the source of natural and moral order. As living and intelligent beings, these gods are moral beings motivated by goodness as they govern the world. Their justice cannot be compromised and they cannot be flattered or bribed by prayers, sacrifices, or other acts of piety. True human piety, for Plato, consists in imitating the rationality and goodness of the gods, not in seeking worldly benefits. Each person may be small in terms of the entire scheme of things; nevertheless, they should remember that they are taking part in a great enterprise by cooperating with the gods. In this way, individuals share in realizing the purpose of the universe and, thereby, find meaning and purpose in their own lives.

Belief in God or the gods is, for Plato, an important factor in the human community since the concept of God undergirds an objective morality and also gives a serious dimension to the moral life through a system of sanctions. However, belief in God (gods), for Plato, is not a matter of faith but the outcome of careful reasoning. In *Laws*, Plato warns against the influence of skeptics and doubters. Doubters should keep their views to themselves. Should they publicly express their views, the ruling Council should condemn them to death. In the end, Plato doubts that human goodness is possible without some grounding in the concept of God. The laws of the city or nation must reflect divine purposes and these laws are reinforced by a sense of the ultimate divine justice. Here we find similarities not only to the Hebrew prophets' proclamations of Yahweh's rule over human history but also the working out of Karma in Far Eastern thought. For Plato—always the philosopher and never the theologian—all such beliefs must be grounded in reason.

Plato on the Fulfilled Life

I have maintained that any moral theory must involve a view of a truly fulfilling human life. For Plato, this truly fulfilling life is one directed by reason while the soul is in its material "prison," the human body. Plato warned that such a life will face challenges, and the rational person may be abused by the rabble and the ignorant. This was the case of Socrates, the Platonist "saint," who was condemned to death by the Athenian rabble. In spite of such challenges, Plato believed that the good and rational person can withstand abuse and live with a sense of self-respect and confidence. It is as though those who punish the truly good "do not know what they do."

After a life directed by reason, the soul will return to the unchanging realm of the Forms and can eternally contemplate the beauty of the Forms. This is Plato's view of heavenly bliss and is reformulated in later Christian thought in terms of the bliss of the beatific vision of God. Plato at times referred to the "Isle of the Blessed," where good men go after death. Death, however, also holds the possibility of imprisonment in Tartarus, where the soul undergoes a variety of punishments. The severity of these punishments depended on the nature of the transgressions enacted while embodied. While some souls will be released, incurably evil souls may be destined to suffer eternally. The example of these suffering souls could cast fear into the hearts of persons contemplating their destiny. Here we find the themes of delayed gratification as well as delayed punishment commonly expressed in world religions.

Plato on Moral Obligation

Any moral theory, I have maintained, must also address the question of possible obligations to others as the individual seeks their own personal fulfillment. Plato addresses this issue in the context of his political philosophy wherein he asserts that a just and harmonious city-state is essential for the fulfillment of its citizens. A just citizen will place the security and harmony of the state above their own individual aspirations. In this commitment, the citizen finds their own fulfillment. Socrates served as a model of the just citizen since he refused to save his own life by escaping from

Athens. Even if the laws of the city led to his execution, Socrates held that these laws must still be honored. Loyalty to the state and its laws was a central characteristic of a rational human being, for Plato. In turn, the state should function for the benefit of all, not of just a few. A well-governed state aims for the happiness of the city as a whole as far as possible.

Plato develops his theory about a well-governed state in his *Republic*. A just state should be ruled by reason as a just soul is to be ruled by reason. A city is made up of a variety of persons with personal needs and talents; therefore, the needs of the city and its people must be met by the abilities of its various citizens. There will be the need for food, clothing, shelter, arts, defense, and governing authority. It follows, then, that these needs will be met by classes of persons who have the appropriate skills for the various tasks. A class of producers will meet the basic needs of food, clothing, and shelter. This class is analogous to the desiring element of the human soul.

Another class, the guardians—analogous to the spirited element of the human soul—would be responsible for defense and the internal order of the city. Finally, the elite class—analogous to reason in the human soul—will be rulers of the state. These rulers would be drawn from the ranks of the most highly trained guardians. We find, here, the famous call for "the Philosopher King."

In theory, Plato held that all persons have the opportunity to reach the level of the ruling class; nevertheless, individuals will reach only the level for which they have the needed capacities. Plato thought it would be necessary to construct a "noble lie" or a "convenient lie" that would help persons accept the class into which they fall. This noble lie would assert that God fashioned human souls from a variety of elements. Some are made of gold, some of silver, and some of iron and brass. We find, here, the three classes: rulers, guardians, and producers. The traits were not, however, strictly inherited since the children of the lower classes could be gifted children who could attain a higher class position. While Plato shared the common view that women are not as physically strong as men, nevertheless, he held that women have the right to attain various levels, including that of guardians and rulers.

Plato also held that some persons are natural slaves, though this was a slavery based on abilities, not on force. Persons with low level of gifts are not able to make wise decisions about the state or about their own lives, so others need to care for them—in much the same way as we care for little children and working animals such as horses.

The responsibility toward others, for Plato, is worked out by the role the person has within the state. The flourishing of the state is a central concern, and the responsibility of the citizen is that of allegiance to the state and its laws. Plato reflects a conservative "law and order" perspective. While the state is rightly concerned about each individual, human beings, in general, are not considered to be equal in a well-governed state. Citizens of enemy states are to be resisted by force. Loving your enemy would be highly irrational from Plato's perspective. There is little in Plato that would suggest a broader vision of the human community such as that developed by the later Stoics. A wise ruler, for Plato, would be one who seeks to live in harmony with other states. Nevertheless, the wise ruler must be prepared to guard the frontiers and interests of the state.

In summary, Plato argued that we have the responsibility of aiding others in their quest for a fulfilled life only within the context of the state or organized community. In this state individuals fill out their roles and gain the advantages or disadvantages implied by their roles. The quest for pleasure would not be the legitimate aim of a fulfilled and rational life. This is in sharp contrast to Epicurus. Instead, each of us, in whatever class, must be committed to living out our lives as workers, guardians, or rulers in those ways that enhance the security and general welfare of the community. If we manage to be fully rational, we can hope that our souls—our essential selves—will find a more complete and lasting fulfillment by rejoining the realm of the Forms and contemplating truth and beauty eternally. In later Christian thought, this fulfillment is transmuted into the beatific vision of God. Maimonides (1138–1204 CE), the influential Jewish philosopher, also viewed the afterlife in the presence of God in somewhat Platonic terms.

Aristotle (384–323 BCE)

Enrolling in Plato's Academy at seventeen, Aristotle spent twenty years as Plato's student. After appearing to accept most of Plato's teaching in his early years as a student, Aristotle broke with his teacher on many significant issues. He rejected Plato's theory of the Forms and developed a less religious view of the universe. He developed a moral theory based on his view of human nature and dispensed with anything like divine sanctions. He developed a more naturalistic view of the universe and made major contributions to the science of his day. The logic he invented remains largely intact to this day.

Aristotle's God

While Aristotle developed a number of arguments for the existence of God—some borrowed from Plato—his view of God radically differed from the developing theisms of Judaism, Christianity and Islam. He had no need to invoke a concept of God for the creation of the universe since he believed that the universe was eternal. He did not need the concept of God to explain the workings of nature since he believed the world of sensory experience could lead to explanations in terms of basic natural causes. He did not need the concept of a God to provide a foundation for morality or as a provider of sanctions for moral failure since he based his moral theory on a view of human nature. Finally, since Aristotle denied that individual human souls exist in any meaningful way beyond the death of the body, he had no need of a God to provide reward or punishment beyond death.

Aristotle did use the idea of God, in part, to explain motion in the heavens and on earth. With many of his day, he assumed that the natural state of any object would be to be at rest. If an object moved, something must have caused it to move. Aristotle had to account for celestial and terrestrial motion. This led to his argument for God as the *Prime Mover* itself unmoved. This God had no interest in the universe. However, the world soul had a yearning—an *eros*—for the beauty of this Prime Mover, and this yearning resulted in celestial motion which, in turn, led to terrestrial motion. Love, as it were, makes the world go around. Even though Aristotle's thought led to the development of science, he reverted to myth or poetry for some of his explanations.

Aristotle's God was perfect, hence unmoving since movement or change would indicate lack of perfection. His god is eternal and incorporeal—without body—and non-material. "The essential quality of God is life, the best of all lives lived eternally without fatigue."[41] Since, for Aristotle, the highest activity of life is thought, the activity of this eternal God is thought. Furthermore, since this God is perfect he thinks only perfect thoughts. But perfect thoughts must be about perfection. This leads to the conclusion that this perfect God thinks about himself—the only perfect object.

> [God] has no impressions, no sensations, no appetites, no will in the sense of desire, no feelings in the sense of passions; he is pure intelligence.... He is free from pain and passion, and is supremely happy. He is everything that a philosopher longs to be.[42]

This God represents an ideal type of existence for the entire universe and for human individuals.

Aristotle's Soul Theory

For Aristotle, the soul is a life principle that moves the body and gives the body its form. However, body and soul are a living unity. There is no life without the soul aspect and no soul without a body. For Aristotle, all life is embodied life, with the exception of his God. Living things have a variety of souls, and the human soul is the most complex. The human soul has the capacity of reason that enables the person to think about the whence, why, and whither of things. Animal and plant souls do not have this capacity. This rational dimension of the human soul appears to be an aspect of the divine mind that comes into the soul from without. The human soul, however, does not have an immortal aspect as in Plato's view. Since there is a body-soul unity, when the body dies, the soul no longer exists. If personal fulfillment is to be achieved, it must take place within the scope of embodied existence. There is no fulfillment—or punishment—beyond death.

Aristotle's Moral Theory

Human beings had long noted that acorns have a way of becoming oaks, and babies have a way of becoming adults. All that seems natural, but what explains such phenomena? Science currently explains this by invoking DNA as a guiding process. Aristotle—anticipating DNA?—suggested that all things have within them some distinctive "end" or "function." Thus everything has its *entelechy* in that it has its own purpose within itself. What, than, might be the end or purpose of a human being? For Aristotle, this end or purpose is linked to his theory that all human art, inquiry and action aims at some good. What, then, is the "good" at which human action and inquiry aim?

To understand the good at which human action aims, Aristotle maintains that we must first understand the distinctive function of human nature. Just as a "good" hammer is one which functions well as a hammer, even so a good human being is one who functions well as a human being. For Aristotle, a "good" man is properly called an "excellent" man, just as a good hammer is an excellent hammer. It will come as no surprise to learn that, for Aristotle, the distinctive function of a man is his capacity to reason.

The good life, the excellent life, is a life characterized by rational actions which aim at the proper end. That proper and final end, for Aristotle, is that of *eudaemonia*, a term translated variously as "happiness" or "flourishing." This happiness, however, is not attained through a quest for pleasure, as Epicurus taught. Nor is flourishing or happiness to be understood as selfishness or self-seeking. There is a strong element of altruism in Aristotle's thought. His excellent man will act in the interests of others and is willing to serve his people and his country. This excellent man would also seek to build a state with institutions that establish justice and fairness. This justice is always expressed within some type of political arrangements, and man, by nature, is a political animal. A successful state is one which helps the lives of its people through basic human needs, but the highest function of the state is to enable its citizens to attain excellence as far as possible.

The depth and subtlety of Aristotle's ethics and his analysis of the nature of virtues cannot be adequately explored in this work. Such an exploration would include his employment of the famous "golden mean" in the characterization of various virtues. (Courage, for example, would be the golden mean between cowardice and foolhardiness.) Nevertheless, the aspects of his thought that have been presented enable us to understand his answers to the two questions which any moral theory must address: 1) What constitutes a truly fulfilling human life? 2) What obligations do we have regarding others who are also pursuing a fulfilled life?

For Aristotle, the fulfilled life—the flourishing life—must be achieved in our mortal, embodied life since there is no meaningful personal existence beyond death. Furthermore, this fulfilled life must be achieved by expressing the exercise of reason—the highest aspect of our human nature. The excellent life is expressed by living honorably, nobly, and loyally within one's community. In this community, certain men should be rulers while others are confined to a life of labor. He also believed women are naturally inferior and some human beings are "slaves by nature." Aristotle was an aristocrat (the word linkage is clear), and he defended aristocracy. There is nothing in his worldview that would call for a more egalitarian perspective.

In his description of an excellent man, Aristotle notes that while short persons may have well-proportioned bodies, they can never be truly beautiful. Furthermore, the truly excellent and appropriately proud man should have a deep voice. Aristotle clearly believed that some human beings are superior to others and that any community should recognize and honor that fact.[43]

Regarding the question of obligations toward others, Aristotle would assert that friendship and family life have a significant place in the life of an excellent man. However, there is no call for a general concern for all human beings or an egalitarian love for individual human beings as equally deserving respect and care. Persons who prove to be excellent are to be treated with the honor and respect they rightly deserve. Women deserve respect appropriate to their proper role. Slaves "by nature" are to receive respect in relation to their role as slaves. Equal rights are given to those who are equal, and unequal rights are for those who are unequal. The truly fulfilled and happy man of reason recognizes these distinctions and addresses each individual in ways appropriate to their status and capacities.

Augustine (354–430)

Born in North Africa, Augustine shaped Christian thought more than any other non-biblical writer. With a pagan father and a Christian mother, Augustine searched for a satisfying worldview. He had early interest in the ontological dualism of the Manicheans and later became attracted to Neoplatonic philosophy. After a conversion experience in his early thirties, he was baptized by Bishop Ambrose of Milan. This work will not attempt to explore the range of his work. Instead, the focus will be on how Augustine links his moral teachings to his theistic worldview. Of particular interest will be how his worldview led him to one of the shortest moral precepts ever proposed: "Love, and do what you like."[44]

The theistic worldview described in Chapter 1 is clearly reflected in Augustine's thought. Indeed, in many ways he was instrumental in the formulation of this worldview. While accepting the Christian canon of scripture as revealed truth, Augustine borrowed abundantly from the heritage left by Plato and the Neoplatonists in constructing his philosophical theology. Augustine shared with them the conviction that the proper moral pathway leads to personal fulfillment.

The Universal Quest for Happiness

According to Augustine, all human beings are created in such a way as to naturally seek happiness. "All men love happiness. . . . For the sake of driving away unhappiness and obtaining happiness, all men do what they do, good or bad."[45] In this assertion, there is a suggestion of psychological egoism, a theory that often appears in philosophical literature. This quest for happiness was not only rational but was also a sign and symptom of the incompleteness and finitude of human beings. However, for Augustine it was crucial to seek this happiness in a correct and fruitful way. This was to be found in the life of love. He draws on the teachings of Jesus and the writings of Saint Paul for this perspective.

The Centrality of Love

According to Gospel accounts, Jesus held that the first and great commandment in Jewish Law was to love God. Reflecting this first commandment, the second commandment was to love the neighbor as oneself.[46] Saint Paul reflected this theme in his assertion that "love is the fulfilling of the Law."[47] This Pauline focus became central for Augustine in his view of *ordered love*. There are many possible objects for our love that meet various human needs, he observed. These needs involve various objects including things, other persons, and one's own self. Therefore, all of these are potentially legitimate objects or relationships of love. Most of all, however, is the need for God. Indeed, the need to love God is the deepest human need and an essential aspect of human nature. When this deepest need is satisfied, the person is freed from the love of illusory goods and misleading adventures. In loving the Highest, one is released from bondage to the lower. Only by loving God does one discover how to properly love objects, other persons, and the self. In the common life, properly ordered love finds its expression in service to the community. Finally, while Augustine sees human evil as the product of an act of the free will, the capacity to love is not a product of human free will but a gift of God's grace. God gives what God commands.

In summary, the truly fulfilling life, for Augustine, is that properly ordered life of love which brings true happiness eventuating in eternal happiness through the resurrection and the final beatific vision of God. As do all moral systems, Augustine's reflects various sanctions for moral failure including a dissatisfying life on earth and an eternal hell for those not elected by God for salvation. God is both boundlessly merciful and severely just. In his later years, Augustine supported the doctrine of double predestination holding that God elects those who will be saved and also selects those who will be damned. Finally, Augustine rejoices in the grace given by God and responds by living out a life of love. In this he reflects the position of John 4:19: "We love, because He first loved us."

A long history of theological debate grew out of Augustine's conclusion of double predestination. Thomas Aquinas developed a finely nuanced version of Augustine's position. The two major Protestant Reformers, John Calvin and Martin Luther, followed Augustine with Calvin presenting the harshest view of the matter. Roman Catholic Church Councils rejected double predestination, and some Protestants rejected predestination in its entirety.

With this vision of the truly fulfilling life, how would Augustine respond to the question of obligations to others who are also seeking the fulfilled life? The answer lies in the focus on the ethic of love involving two central implications. First, his ethic and faith implies a universalism that rejects any form of tribalism exalting one group over another. All human beings are to be loved without distinction. Second, such love seeks to care for the basic human needs of others, especially those without wealth or power or voice. Furthermore, since human needs include primarily the need to love God, bringing others into the faith would be an act of love. Yet those who remain outside the faith are not to be abused or rejected. With what appears to be a proper element of caution, Augustine leaves the ultimate fate of those outside of the faith in the hands of God.

Thomas Aquinas (1225–71)

While Augustine synthesized theology and philosophy by linking Christian faith to Plato's thought, Aquinas produces his highly influential works by linking Christian faith to Aristotle's philosophy. Since opponents to Christianity were using Aristotle's philosophy as a means of refuting Christian faith, Aquinas, in his early years, set out to show why Aristotle was mistaken. Upon studying Aristotle, however, Aquinas decided he could join the Greek, in part, rather than refute him. Influenced by Augustine, Aquinas also drew from many earlier writers, including ancient Greeks, Muslims and Jews. Central to this exploration of the thought of Aquinas will be his view of what constitutes a truly fulfilling life and the nature of obligation toward others. His theistic worldview was described in Chapter 1.

Aquinas and Aristotle

Aquinas agreed with Aristotle on several issues. He accepted Aristotle's contention that human beings naturally and appropriately seek happiness.

Furthermore, Aquinas accepts and builds upon Aristotle's claim that morality involves the quest for happiness and that in order to achieve such happiness a person must fulfill their end as a human being. Both held that human beings, like animals, have appetites, passions and sensations linked to the physical body. Both held that human reason ought to control such appetites in order to achieve happiness; also, both held that the natural virtues of courage, temperance, justice, and prudence result when the appetites are controlled by reason.

However, while Aristotle thought only in terms of a natural end or aim for a human being, Aquinas added a supernatural end that was the Beatific vision of God realized in heaven. To achieve that end, Aquinas held that human beings require supernatural revelation to become aware not only of that high end but also the supernatural means of attaining that end. Such revelation, for Aquinas, comes through the Scriptures. In his philosophical theology, Aquinas consistently claimed that faith is not in opposition to reason but adds to it.

Aquinas on Law: Eternal, Natural, Divine

The moral pathway described by Aquinas included *Eternal Law*, *Natural Law*, and *Divine law*. For Aquinas, God as creator is the ultimate authority of all things natural and moral. The entire universe is governed by Divine Reason, which Aquinas identifies as Eternal Law. Natural Law is that aspect of Eternal Law that provides the basis for moral obligations. This Natural Law can be rationally discerned by examining the very nature of human life and the world. These laws are linked directly to human nature as created by God and are reflected in a variety of inclinations, For instance, persons have a natural tendency to protect their own lives, which implies that suicide would be opposed to the Natural Law to sustain life. Suicide, for Aquinas, was a moral sin. Another example relates to human sexuality and reproduction. He argued that reproduction is a natural human inclination and forms the basis for the moral expression of marriage. Since the propagation of the species is, for Aquinas, the natural end of sexual union, any attempt to deliberately frustrate that end would be in opposition to Natural Law. This implies that artificial means of birth control would be immoral. This view of Natural Law has left a major imprint on Roman Catholic moral teachings to this day.

The Necessity of Divine Law

While human reason can discern Natural Law, Aquinas held that Divine Law is needed to ensure the supernatural end of human existence. This Divine Law, however, cannot be discerned directly by human reason but is gifted to humankind as an act of God's grace. Here Aquinas disagrees sharply with Aristotle, who held that human reason is the adequate basis for the moral life. While the natural virtues of courage, temperance, justice, and prudence are significant, Aquinas argued that the theological virtues of faith, hope, and love are needed for salvation. These virtues are not achieved by way of human effort or natural abilities but are "infused" into the person by God's grace. These theological virtues are essential for the attainment of the Beatific Vision. All this directly implies that salvation is, ultimately, a gift from God and cannot be attained by human effort on its own. Following Augustine, Aquinas held that God gives what God requires. In this, Aquinas asserts a form of predestination by arguing that the Beatific Vision of God results entirely because of God's gift of unmerited grace. Those not gifted with this grace remain eternally condemned. This doctrine of unmerited grace underlies the crucial role of the church in traditional Roman Catholic thought since the church mediates the grace between God and the faithful Christian. A variety of influential voices—including Aquinas—held that there is no salvation outside of the church. The sacraments of the church are means of grace. To be outside of the church is to be without access to this saving grace. This dogma carries with it the heavy weight of possible excommunication from the church.

Aquinas on Morality

The Christian theism of Aquinas led him to a moral vision strikingly different from that of Aristotle's naturalism. True human fulfillment, for Aquinas, is to be found through the pathway of faith and morality that leads, finally, to the beatific vision of God in heaven. For Aristotle, since individual existence ends with death, human fulfillment was to be gained by achieving human excellence in earthly life through the applications of reason. During the earthly journey, the model of Christian humility and service proposed by Aquinas is in sharp contrast to the "excellent man" of Aristotle with his self-sufficiency, independence, and elitist tendencies of contempt for lesser human beings.

Happiness as the Aim

Aquinas agreed with Aristotle that happiness, in some form, is the appropriate aim of the human venture. They also agree that straying from the pathway resulted in sanctions. For Aristotle the sanction for failing to be an excellent person would be a lack of happiness in this life. This would be so, even if the person ignorantly believed their life was a happy life. Only the truly rational man can discern the difference. The sanctions, for Aquinas, appear to be more serious since eternal sanctions beyond death are part of the scene he envisioned. The morally corrupt person in this life may appear to be living the happy life, according to Aquinas. However, since all human beings are alienated from God because of original sin, those not gifted with God's grace remain alienated and spend eternity in some sort of suffering. For Aquinas, God's grace is irresistible when given, but God's justice is stern.

Obligations to Others

Regarding the believer's obligations to others, Aquinas took a generally egalitarian position. Love (*caritas*) is to be expressed to all human beings since they all have souls with a divine destiny. This love, however, must be an expression of the natural law as well as the divine law. Both laws are descriptive and prescriptive of the pathway of graced faith that leads to the Beatific Vision of God. The difficulties, here, are in the details that cannot be developed in this brief overview.

The state, for Aquinas, was an essential aspect of the basic nature of the human life. He also believed that the political sovereign derived his authority from God. As creator and sustainer, God is not only the ultimate power, but also the ultimate authority in all things. Authority, in effect, runs from the top down. The primary responsibility of the state is to look after the common good of its citizens. This would include keeping peace, pursuing harmony among its people, providing resources for sustaining life, and preventing obstacles to the good life. The state rules its citizens through law, but such rule must reflect justice as a reflection of natural law. Any law enacted by the state that runs counter to the general principles of natural law does not bind the citizen and should not be observed. In shaping the moral pathway for citizens, the church has authority over the state just as God has authority over the church. While many details of civil law are left to the decisions of the state—such as how to punish criminals—the principles of natural law and divine law are the final standards. Aquinas also argued that the state should not attempt to create a civil law to enforce every natural law since such attempts could result in more harm than good to the human community. In this, Aquinas recognized the limitations of human insight and goodness. In this fallen world, the human community is not able to reach anything like a new Eden.

The Role of the State

The state, for Aquinas, has the responsibility of preventing obstacles to the good life. In this way, the state is subordinate to the church in the sphere of the ultimate and supernatural ends of human beings. In practice, this implies that the state must guard against heresies that endanger the eternal destiny of human souls. In his *Summa Theologica*, Aquinas asserts, "If forgers and malefactors are put to death by secular power, there is much more reason for excommunicating and even of putting to death one convicted of heresy."[48] Here the Saint reflects a theological tribalism often reflected in monotheistic traditions. Following Aristotle, he also echoed the long established tradition of male superiority. Women, he suggested, are naturally defective and are "by nature subordinate to man, because the power of rational discernment is by nature stronger in man. . . . [Women] are not tough enough to withstand their longings."[49]

Thomas Hobbes (1588–1679)

An example of an early modern mind, Hobbes broke with the past and embraced the new natural science of Copernicus and Galileo. In doing so, he developed a thoroughly materialistic and mechanical approach to philosophy. He believed that the methods of geometry could be fruitful in the search for truth. Born in the year the Spanish Armada was defeated off the coast of England, Hobbes mirrors the violence of his times. Central to his views of ethics and politics was his conviction that the fear of death, especially violent death, prompted many human activities.

Hobbes on Human Nature

His view of human nature is starkly presented in his claim that in the state of nature, where there is no civil government, there would be perpetual war of all against all, and life would be "solitary, nasty, brutish and short." Furthermore, in this state of nature morality would not exist nor would there be any concern for the needs of others. Even when living in a more established and abiding state, human beings would still be primarily concerned about their own survival. For Hobbes, man is a "ferocious animal" caught up in enmity, competition, and war in the quest for life, riches, honor, and power. This belief about human nature is not far from the view of "fallen" humanity held by the Protestant Reformers, John Calvin and Martin Luther. Clearly a psychological egoist, Hobbes believed that human activity is always motivated by self-centered needs and desires. Thus, when persons exercise their "will," they are merely carrying out the causal effects of their own appetites and aversions. Furthermore, they equate goodness with their own desires. How, then, did God and morality fit into this philosophical scheme of things?

Hobbes on Religion

Hobbes wrote at length on a variety of religious topics, but it is difficult to know just what his own personal opinions might have been. Because of his interest in ethics and politics, he was forced to deal with matters religious since religion was largely inseparable from the politics and ethics of his day. He granted that there is a God whose existence can be proven in terms of causes; however, he also claimed that we do not and cannot know *what* this God might be. All religious claims, therefore, needed to be analyzed and critiqued by reason. He also believed that such analysis and critique yielded little by way of knowledge. In the end, consistent with his emphasis on the absolute authority of the ruler of the state, he left religious matters largely in the hands of the ruling authority at that time. Finally, he made no meaningful connection between religious doctrines and moral behavior. His political philosophy and its ethical implications were solely grounded in philosophy with no connection to religious belief.

Hobbes on Morality and Rights

Hobbes had little to say specifically about morality. His major interest was political philosophy where he discussed questions about human actions and behavior. His famous defense of the absolute power of the sovereign was grounded in his view of human nature. Fearful of death and pursuing security, power, and wealth, a rational person, Hobbes believed, would "seek peace and pursue it." Such peace would be possible, he argued, only with a powerful ruling authority. Without the existence of such a power that could control behavior through fear of punishment, Hobbes held that each person has a "natural right" to do what he pleases to whomever he pleases. However, a person's natural right to do what they please does not obligate others to allow that person the freedom to do so. To have a "right" in this sense is equivalent to "having the power." Thus, the lion in the African jungle has the right to do as it pleases. However, this right could be restrained by the power of other lions or animals.

This natural right in the human sphere, Hobbes observed, results in the "war of all against all," a situation no rational person would desire. Through extended arguments, Hobbes shows that the rational man would be willing to give up his natural right if others would do the same. But the citizen sets this natural right aside if—and only if—the sovereign power takes on the responsibility of protecting that citizen from others. There is a strong "law and order" theme in Hobbes.

This transfer of rights is considered to be a contract and establishes a duty to abide by the contract. The task of the sovereign—the great Leviathan—is to make certain through the use of power that such contracts are honored. In the absence of such a power, contracts would be "mere words" with little hope of being respected. Furthermore, in the absence of such a power, there would be little assurance of either peace or safety. We can appreciate Hobbes's argument if we imagine, for instance, New York City or Chicago without a government or police force even for a few days.

Hobbes on Peace and Justice

There would be no peace without such a sovereign power, Hobbes believed, nor would there be any meaningful concept of justice. For Hobbes, the terms "just" and "unjust" held meaning only when there is sufficient government power to compel persons to abide by their contracts and agreements for fear of punishment. Without the threat of a coercive power, contracts could not be considered valid, and the very idea of justice would be empty of meaning. The lion in the state of nature, for instance, cannot be reasonably accused of being unjust. With the coercive power of ruler, just acts would not be punished while unjust acts would be. For Hobbes, the rational person is always guided by prudence, and with an absolute sovereign enforcing the laws, it would be prudent to be law-abiding.

Hobbes often wrote about "laws of nature," and even "moral laws" and "divine laws." However, in the end he reduced these concepts to rational maxims about how persons can best achieve their own security and aspirations in the generally competitive and hostile human world. Such maxims have little meaningful connection to theological convictions or to the essential human nature that Aquinas proposed. Hobbes clearly dismissed the traditional natural law theory, as held by Aquinas, which held that certain binding moral laws can be rationally discerned from created nature. For this and other elements of his thought, Hobbes became the most frequently attacked philosopher of his day.

In Summary

In summary, Hobbes had little to say directly about what constitutes a truly fulfilling life. Even given a society ruled by an all powerful sovereign, Hobbes held no rosy expectations about human existence. The most we can hope for and work for, he believed, is a condition of peace with others that grants us some possibility to pursue our own quest for power, honor, and riches. Life would be satisfying to the degree that such desires are satisfied. Hobbes neither hoped for glorious fulfillment in Heaven, nor did he appear to fear punishment in Hell.

Given his basic assumption that we are always—and necessarily—motivated by self-concern alone, Hobbes sets aside any claim that we have something like a moral obligation to aid others in their quest for a fulfilled life. Instead, a truly rational person would pursue their own self-interest and would help others only when such aid serves self-interest. We find, here, a view similar to that of "reciprocal altruism" that is currently discussed in evolutionary psychology. In the end, Hobbes would have us understand that a human being, always a "ferocious animal," may still, as a rational creature, "seek peace and pursue it."

David Hume (1711–76)

Generally considered by his friends as a good and kind but tough-minded man, David Hume threw out his philosophical gauntlet in the closing lines of his *Enquiry Concerning Human Understanding*:

> If we take in our hand any volume; of divinity or school metaphysics, for instance; let us ask, *Does it contain any abstract reasoning concerning quantity or numbers?* No. "*Does it contain any experimental reasoning concerning matters of fact and existence*" No. Commit it then to the flames; for it can contain nothing but sophistry and illusion.[50]

In summary, Hume's point is that objects of knowledge are of two kinds: relations of ideas and matters of fact. Relations of ideas, as in abstract reasoning, involves knowledge that is not derived from sensory experience. The truths of geometry and mathematics would be examples. We may, by way of sensory experience, learn that two plus two equals four, but the truth of that proposition is not based on sensory experience. Instead, its truth is based on the very meanings of the words or symbols—relations of ideas. Modern logicians refer to such propositions as analytic wherein the predicate of the proposition does not tell us anything new about the subject. For example, "A brother is a male sibling." So, also, "Two plus two equals four." Thus, analytic propositions do not express "matters of fact" which are derived from sensory experience. Propositions that purport to express a matter of fact are termed "synthetic." In propositions of this sort, the predicate *does* tell us something new about the subject, as in "That cat is calico" or "Some crows are white, although most crows are black." In making his claim, Hume is expressing the empiricist view that factual knowledge about the world is derived only from sensory experience.

Hume on Knowledge of God

This basic claim about human knowledge yields philosophical fruit—or, perhaps, lack of fruit—when Hume addresses religious or moral issues. Propositions, such as "God exists," are generally considered to be synthetic since they purport to make some factual claim about the world. For Hume, however, "God exists" fails to be a knowledge claim since he believed that no sensory experience can lead to that conclusion. His *Dialogues on Natural Religion* is noted for its sustained attack on attempts to prove the existence of God. For Hume, belief in God is never a matter of knowledge, but of faith in something like divine revelation. Furthermore, he would not have considered himself to be a man of faith.

Hume on Moral Knowledge

Hume makes a similar claim about moral knowledge. Just as propositions about God are beyond the range of human knowledge, so also are claims about moral knowledge. To assert that some action is "morally good" is not to make some factual statement about the action, Hume argues. He points out that one can examine such an action from every angle and yet perceive nothing that we can label as "good." We may see someone binding a wound, or helping an aged person across the street, or feeding some starving child; but in no way do we see "goodness." To discover the meaning of "goodness," Hume argues, we must examine our feelings. To call some action "good" reveals that we have a sentiment of approval regarding that action. Our feelings, not our reason or sensory experience, are the basis for our moral judgments.

Furthermore, Hume asserts, reason alone never moves us to some action. We act only when we believe that the action will yield some result that we desire. In this sense, says Hume, "Reason is and ought only to be the slave of the passions."[51] Our reason cannot tell us what we *ought* to want. It can tell us how to get *what* we want. Thus, no matter of fact, by itself, can ever lead to some moral judgment or conclusion. The *fact* that the bite of a rattle snake might kill you leads to action only if we *desire* not to be killed. Hume follows his empiricist position regarding knowledge to its logical conclusion. Since knowledge of fact can be derived only from sensory experience (sight, sound, smell, etc.), and since we have no sensory experience which identifies "goodness," the judgment of goodness must be the results of our feelings.

Hume's Explanation of Morality

Nevertheless, Hume does not ignore morality or reject its significance in human relations. Ethics was a major interest and Hume hoped to bring clarity to the field just as Galileo and Newton had done in their scientific fields. This clarity was to be achieved by relying on facts and observations. In his *Enquiry Concerning the Principles of Morals*, Hume sought to *explain* the nature of morality rather than give us moral advice. His explanation is rooted in the claim that the human sentiment of sympathy or "fellow-feeling" is the spring from which moral judgments flow. A virtuous action is not one that reflects obedience to some moral law or rule. Indeed, he held that the very idea of moral rules as some aspect of objective truth "can never be made intelligible." There are, for Hume, no moral laws or virtues expounded by God or inherent in human nature that *reason* can discover. This claim is in sharp contrast to the Natural Law claim of Aquinas. Instead, he defines virtue to be "whatever action or quality gives to a spectator the pleasing sentiment of approbation, and vice the contrary."[52]

Hume guards against reducing ethics to purely subjective or relative terms, like some matter of taste, by claiming that moral sentiments are a natural part of all human beings. The sense of sympathy or fellow-feeling is a principle widely expressed in human nature. Human beings from every age and culture also express the same sense of approval for deeds which are brave, generous or noble, even when such deeds may be harmful to their own particular self-interest. A brave deed done by some soldier is worthy of praise even if it harms our own cause. But, Hume continues, we praise certain actions precisely because we see them as useful and agreeable to *someone's* interests.

Hume Gives no Moral Advice

Hume carefully avoids telling us what we *ought* to do, for that would imply that there is some moral rule that should be honored. Instead, he *describes* how human beings generally feel about actions that are useful and agreeable. Furthermore, given his claim that no fact, by itself, can ever entail a value or a motive, he cannot logically claim to give us moral advice. Hume never argues: "Since human beings generally have feelings of sympathy for others, therefore we *should* act sympathetically toward others." Just as he would not argue that since human beings generally feel hostile toward those who abuse them, they *ought* to take revenge on that person.

Natural inclinations do not in themselves provide moral guidelines though these inclinations may be part of the cause of our actions. Nor does it follow in some deterministic way that if we feel sympathy toward others, we will, therefore, *act* on such feelings. We may honor our enemy's wit and bravery, but that fact will not necessarily lead us to act in a benevolent way toward our enemy. We still must decide just how we will act to pursue our own wants, needs, and desires that will conflict with those of our enemy. While we may have some sense of sympathy for another person, our own self-interests will be the "passion" which directs our reason and responses.

The Place of Sympathy in Hume's Thought

Hume's emphasis on sympathy and fellow-feeling softens the stark psychological egoism that Hobbes proposed. Still, the altruistic inclinations Hume describes do not over-rule natural self-interest. The good may involve altruism, but the most we can reasonably hope for, in Hume's own words, is "confined generosity." This is the language of self-referential altruism. The primary aim of our actions is our own well-being, or the well-being of those we love, or the well-being of those with whom we are linked through some type of identification—clan, faith, nation, ethnicity. In the tussle for the perceived goods of life, we will side with "our own" not with "the other." This observation serves to underline the persistent issue in moral philosophy: "Are there ever moral reasons which, at times, properly trump reasons of prudence and self-referential altruism?" Hume did not think so.

Belief in God, for Hume, has no legitimate place in moral reflection. Not only is knowledge of God impossible, religious beliefs that God provides moral guidance and also protects our interests are only a form of infantilism. Hume certainly shows disdain for "celibacy, fasting, penance, mortification, self-denial, humility, silence, solitude, and the whole train of monkish virtues."[53]

Hume on the Fulfilled Life

The nature of the fulfilled life, as Hume conceived it, reflects a secular view of morality with an emphasis on peace and mutual evaluation, not that of "scolding and mutual reproach." Furthermore, any fulfillment must be sought in this life since Hume rejects any meaningful form of personal immortality beyond death. But the fulfilled life is linked to virtuous living. His list of virtues generally accepted by human beings included good sense, knowledge, wit, eloquence, humanity, fidelity, truth, temperance, and dignity of mind. He would also include justice, honesty, good nature, mercy, gratitude, kindness, tenderness, generosity, sobriety, patience, forethought, and a proud spirit.[54] The Calvinists of Hume's day would not be happy with his list of virtues, nor would monks or generals. Since death ends all experience, any sanctions for moral failure must also take place in this life. The disadvantages, for Hume, for failing to express virtuous living would be a lower level of life's joys and satisfactions,

In spite of his skepticism, his friends found in him many of the virtues he listed. Hume carried his convictions to the grave. In his account of a conversation with the dying Hume, the pious Boswell did not find the repentance he had hoped for from this great skeptic. Hume died peacefully, "remaining immune to the consolations of either theism or immortality."[55]

Immanuel Kant (1724–1804)

"Two things fill my mind with ever new and increasing admiration and awe . . . the starry heavens above and the moral law within." This famous passage from Immanuel Kant suggests his philosophical concerns about the nature of scientific knowledge and the nature of morality. The Protestant Pietism of Kant's parents influenced much of his later thought. This sect put more emphasis on faith as trust, instead of correct doctrine. He traveled little, apparently never leaving the town of Königsberg. Nevertheless, he studied much and wrote volumes of influential works. His disciplined life is reflected in his daily "philosopher's walk" around town that could be timed by his neighbors with great precision.

Hume's writings not only awakened Kant from his "dogmatic slumber" but also threatened to undercut scientific as well as moral knowledge. Kant set out to rescue both from Hume's assault by analyzing how reason itself thinks about the world and about morality. For Kant, reason has both a theoretical as well as a practical function. Theoretical reason discovers what is true about the world, while practical reason provides moral guidance. To paraphrase Galileo, reason shows us how the world goes and also how to go in the world.

Reason in Science

In science, Kant argues that human reason (mind) has certain structures which impose order on the sensory experiences that come from the world "out there." The mind organizes these experiences. This is in sharp contrast to the common view that assumes our mind conforms to the order of the world experienced; what we "see" is the way the world out there really is. For Kant, we do not know what the tree "out there" is "in itself." What we do know is the result of how the mind orders the experiences resulting from sensory contact with the tree. He does assume that the tree is really "out there," not merely some construction of our consciousness—some kind of dream. But all we can know about that tree is our "inner" experience of how our mind orders sensory experience.

With Hume, Kant held that sensory experience does not show us cause-effect relationships in the world. Hume argued that while we see "constant conjunctions" between events we do not see "cause-effect" relationships. We do not really know that some X causes some Y. We do see that Y usually follows X. For Kant, the conclusion that X causes Y is supplied by the mind that orders thought in terms of cause-effect relations. "Cause-effect" is a "category of the mind," not something perceived directly through the senses. Given this analysis, Kant believed that science does, in this way, help us see how the world works in cause-effect ways. The same analysis is applied to space and time which are "forms of intuition" employed by the mind, not actualities observed through the senses.

Reason in Morality

For Kant, mind also played a significant role in his analysis of morality and its possible relationship with the idea of God. With Hume, Kant believed that the existence of God cannot be proven by reason, nor are such things as virtues and goodness discovered by way of sensory experience. But while Hume linked judgments about virtues to our feelings or passions, Kant anchored such judgments in the rational structure of the mind itself. Since we cannot know that God exists, Kant concluded that genuine moral knowledge cannot be based on religious claims. Given that approach, some find it odd that Kant eventually argued that we need to *posit* something like God in order to make sense out of morality.

Central to Kant's analysis of morality is his claim that a morally good action must not only *accord* with duty, but must also be done with duty as its *motive*. For Kant, this just seems to be the way we *think* about morality. The will is good if and only if it does its duty for duty's sake alone. Telling the truth, for instance, is in accord with duty. However, if one's motive for telling the truth is to escape punishment, then that act has no truly moral status. Such an act is not to be construed as immoral, but it has no clear moral standing. An act which accords with duty merely because it "pays" does not constitute a moral action. Telling the truth solely because it is one's *duty* to tell the truth, in spite of consequences, would constitute a truly moral act. Implied in this analysis is a clear distinction between what is done on the basis of inclination or feeling and what is done on the basis of duty. True morality does not spring from our inclinations; indeed, morality may often conflict with our inclinations. Kant clearly has fundamental disagreements with Hume on this matter.

Analysis of "Duty"

How, then, do we recognize what constitutes a duty? In pursuing his answer, Kant developed a rigorous philosophical pathway involving a careful analysis of how we *think* about morality and what we believe about moral obligations. We ask not only "What *shall* I do?" but also "What *ought* I do?" Furthermore, when we think clearly, we realize that what is considered morally right is often quite distinct from our own interests and desires. Conscience, remorse, and the basic awareness of duty attest to the claim that morality has upon us. For Kant, reason's awareness of duty can properly be called the recognition of a moral law. He goes on to argue that the very idea of *law* involves unconditional, not hypothetical, obedience. That is, law does not provide some type of hypothetical claim which states "If you want X, then do Y." Rather, law orders "Do Y because it is your duty to do so." The very idea of law, Kant asserts, implies universality. If law is truly law, it applies to all, everywhere, and at all times. Law is never qualified by a particular set of circumstances or by the special interest of an individual. If the law is law, it applies to all others and to me; I cannot modify law to fit my own particular circumstances or desires.

The Categorical Imperative

Pressing this analysis, Kant finally arrives at his duly famous *categorical imperative*. "Act only according to that maxim whereby you can at the same time will that it should become a universal law."[56] (The phrase, "can at the same time" carries the meaning of "can without inconsistency.") This rule is categorical in that it applies universally to all rational beings. It is imperative in that it states a principle upon which we ought to act. A maxim, for Kant, is any general rule of action. Hence, the categorical imperative asserts that if we act according to some maxim, we must be willing to make that maxim into a universal law that everyone ought to follow. If we are unwilling to will the universality of a rule or maxim, then that rule or maxim falls short of being moral.

Examples: Promises and Lying

Consider, for instance, the practice of making promises. If Joe is tempted to break a promise he had made, he could formulate the maxim: "Break promises when it benefits me." But, Kant asserts, Joe could not will to make that maxim a universal law that would order all persons to break a promise when it rebounds to their benefit. If such a law became universal, promises would be stripped of their very meaning and no one would trust promises made. Hence, Kant concludes, reason shows that promising is possible only if promises are honored. While the plain man may not be able to follow Kant's argument here, Kant is certain that this same plain man understands in his very being that promises are to be kept.

Another example of Kant's rigorous application of moral duty is his illustration regarding lying. For Kant, lying is always morally wrong. If some deranged man comes to your door waving a handgun and asks if your son is at home, the inclination to lie to the gunman would be exceedingly strong. Nevertheless, Kant maintains that lying to the gunman cannot be morally justified. For in lying to the gunman you would be acting on the maxim: "Lie to someone when it redounds to your benefit." However, Kant would argue, that maxim could not be willed to be a universal law since such a law would undercut the very meaning and function of communication. You would never have grounds for believing what others say.

Morality: Not an Imposition from "Outside"

Kant's understanding of the nature of morality implies that our rational nature has its own moral authority. Moral laws are not laid upon us by some outside authority. While a Christian might admire the moral teachings of Jesus, Jesus does not represent, for Kant, some kind of moral guru. Instead, the Christian approves of Jesus's teachings not because Jesus taught them, but because we recognize those teachings as morally sound. "Love of neighbor" is a sound moral maxim, not because Jesus taught it, but because it is consistent with our moral reason.

God and Morality

How, then, does the idea of God fit into Kant's moral philosophy when he maintains that we cannot know that God exists or that some Divine Law has been revealed to us? For Kant, the moral law is *within* as an expression of our nature as rational creatures. Rational creatures think about morality in just the way the Kant has described. Yet the concept of God becomes important for him. Kant argues that the very way we think about morality leads us to the existence of God as a "postulate of practical reason."

He seeks to demonstrate that there is a fundamental connection between virtue and happiness, and that God's existence must be posited to make such a connection.

Kant maintains that an analysis of the way we think about morality yields several insights. First, if we are to be morally responsible, we must be free either to do our duty or to refuse so to do. While freedom of the will cannot be proven by reason, such a freedom must be a "postulate of practical reason" in order to make sense of morality. If the call of duty is to make sense, we must possess freedom of the will. Second, even though the quest for happiness must not be the *motive* for doing our duty, nevertheless, the very idea of morality implies that a truly moral person ought to be rewarded with true happiness. This is a theme in many systems of morality; "Morality pays." Practical reason, then, posits that virtue leads to true happiness. Third, since the moral quality of an action depends upon the purity of the motive that prompts the action (willing the action on the basis of duty), our moral rewards depend upon our *motives*. Fourth, reason tells us that virtue and happiness are necessarily linked; nevertheless, in this earthly life it seems clear that truly moral persons are not rewarded. It follows, then, that there must be a reward of some kind in an existence beyond death. Furthermore, the soul as a rational entity seeks the perfect good—the complete conformity of the will to the call of duty. Since such perfect goodness cannot be attained in this earthly life, it follows that there must be an unending duration of the existence of this rational being. In this way the immortality of the soul is posited.

Moral Reason Posits God

Given those evident truths linked to morality, the existence of God must be posited in order to conceive of a universe compatible with such truths;

for if morality is to be as reason understands it, there must be some Power which: 1) accurately knows our motives in order to link our virtue to our happiness; 2) has the power and wisdom to construct a universe in which virtue and happiness are linked; and 3) has the power and wisdom to provide the scene for an immortal soul to seek its moral perfection. All this leads to the positing of God's existence. Morality, as Kant conceives of it, would be an absurd enterprise from the standpoint of a purely naturalistic worldview. As we shall see later, Friedrich Nietzsche agrees with Kant on this last point and goes on to claim that, with the "death of God," religion-based morality is rendered irrational.

A Circular Argument?

Kant's reasoning, which led him to posit the existence of God, may involve a circular argument. He claimed that reason understands "duty" and "law" in a particularly precise way. These understandings, however, seem to be rooted in systems of religious morality and are not to be found in naturalistic moral systems. Therefore, he needs to posit God's existence in order to justify his original claims about the meanings of "duty" and "law." To put this point in another way, one could claim that what Kant delivers in his analysis of practical reason are, in fact, his own *intuitions* which were rooted in the religious Pietism of his roots. Nevertheless, Kant's enormous influence and his curious use of the idea of God make Kant's philosophy one of particular interest to the argument pursued in this work.

Kant on the Fulfilled Life

Kant's vision of the truly fulfilled life involves this union of virtue with happiness. He believed that, as rational beings, we are fully satisfied only when this union of virtue and happiness is achieved. While Kant expresses a moral rigorism, he despised an asceticism that passed itself off as morality. Happiness has its proper place since the highest good, the *summum bonum*, must include both virtue and happiness. However, while happiness is pleasant for the one who possesses it, morally right behavior is always a necessary condition for its attainment.

Kant argues that it is not possible to express a truly moral will in this world where the struggle between inclination and duty continues. Nevertheless, morality demands that a truly moral will ought to be achieved and is to be understood as the holiness which God's justice requires. The call to moral duty continues, but the immortality of the soul as a postulate of practical reason makes possible a comforting hope for a blessed future.[57] While Kant is spare about the details of such a "blessed future," it is clear that true human fulfillment is not attained in this earthly life.

> Although Kant refers to the "Infinite Being" who imputes to a person perfect virtue even if he has only made progress toward it, there is no mention of fellowship with God or other persons as a source of joy. Happiness is regarded as having its source solely in one's virtue.[58]

Kant on Moral Obligation

Kant links our obligations to others to his view of human beings as rational creatures. In developing implications of the categorical imperative, Kant holds that other persons should not be seen as means to our own ends, but as ends in themselves. Others are not to be used purely for our own interests. If others are used for our own ends in some situations, then the action must also involve seeing the other as ends in themselves. This would render reciprocal altruism as morally acceptable. The employer uses an employee for their own end, but employees must be honored and treated as ends in themselves.

The rule to view others as ends in themselves leads Kant to a variety of conclusions regarding sexuality. In Kant we find a theme that runs through much of our cultural heritage—that our human passions often clash with our rational aspects. In Plato, for instance, our rational soul should direct and guide other non-rational aspects of soul. This theme was linked to be a negative view of the human body, its functions and desires. Plato saw the body as the "prison house" of the soul. Augustine was, for a time, interested in the Manicheans, who held to an ontological dualism between spirit and matter.

In Kant we find that sexuality is suspect since it inclines persons to use others as means to their own ends—that of sexual gratification. Furthermore, masturbation is degrading. Sex within marriage is acceptable, but Kant regarded such as "a merely animal union." Rape, he argued, should be punished with castration. Anyone guilty of bestiality should be banished from society. Kant, himself, never married.

John Stuart Mill (1806–74)

One of the founders of utilitarianism, J. S. Mill caught the attention not only of professional philosophers but also of politicians and ordinary citizens. With its general simplicity and its compatibility with what many people already believed, utilitarianism helped to bring about social and political reform in England. It remains an influential theory to this day. Mill was deeply influenced by Jeremy Bentham, almost sixty years Mill's senior. Bentham, in turn, was influenced by Hume's emphasis on empirical method as well as his psychological analysis of human motives. Bentham hoped to make morality into a science as much as possible. The opening lines of Bentham's *Introduction to the Principles of Morals and Legislation* states his basic claim:

> Nature has placed mankind under the governance of two sovereign masters, pain and pleasure. It is for them alone to point out what we ought to do, as well as to determine what we shall do. On the one hand the standard of right and wrong, on the other the chain of cause and effects, are fastened to their throne. They govern us in all we do, in all we say, in all we think.[59]

Bentham's Psychological Hedonism

These lines carry an open endorsement of psychological hedonism, the theory that people *necessarily* act in ways which promise to bring them pleasure and to avoid pain. Psychological hedonism is a *descriptive* theory in that it purports to describe how persons *do* act, but does not describe how they *ought* to act. Bentham's argument moves from the psychological theory to his principle of utility. From the fact that we *desire* pleasure, we can conclude that we *ought* to pursue pleasure. While Kant argued, "I ought, therefore I can," Bentham appears to argue "I ought, since I can do no other." Although Bentham subscribes to psychological hedonism, he does not endorse an ethic of selfishness. His emphasis was on self-interest, not selfishness, for he was convinced that our own happiness is best achieved by pursuing the general happiness of others. It is in our own self-interest, Bentham believed, to pursue this general happiness.

The Principle of Utility

Bentham's principle of utility—"the greatest happiness for the greatest number"—was formulated as his primary moral principle. Furthermore, "good" is to be understood in terms of happiness or pleasure. Bentham recognized that he could not prove in some deductive or empirical way that happiness is the basis of what is good and right. Nevertheless, he claimed that all other moral principles, when closely analyzed, reduce to the principle of utility. For instance, religiously based moral rules would reduce to his principle since God's reason for providing such rules would be that of producing the greatest happiness for the greatest number. Bentham finally sets the problem of proving the principle aside by asserting,

> Is it susceptible to proof? It should seem not; for that which is used to prove every thing else, cannot itself be proved: a chain of proof must have its commencement somewhere. To give such a proof is as impossible as it is needless.[60]

J. S. Mill's Utilitarianism

In his Utilitarianism, J. S. Mill defends the principle of utility and psychological hedonism expressed by Bentham. However, his own formulation of utilitarianism differs from Bentham's in several ways. Building on his claim that pain and pleasure are the causes of human actions, Bentham argued that a number of sanctions or forms of punishment help to shape human behavior. These sanctions include the physical, political, moral, and religious. Burning my finger on a hot candle flame is a sanction that teaches me to avoid such contact. A jail sentence given to me by a magistrate is a political sanction that teaches me to avoid a life of crime. A neighbor's refusal to assist me because of their dislike of my moral character is a moral sanction that may alter my future behavior. Finally, God's punishment for a sin I committed represents the religious sanction. To these sanctions, Mill adds the internal sanction of conscience, the general sense of duty that exists as a subjective aspect of our nature and influences our actions. He links this to the principle of utility by maintaining that genuine happiness must include that sense of personal affirmation felt by everyone when honoring duty.

This is not, however, "duty for duty's sake." Rather, it is duty for the sake of our own happiness. The pursuit of duty, Mill believed, is a fundamental element in our natural and legitimate quest for happiness. It was this emphasis on the satisfaction derived from duty that led Mill to claim that his utilitarian position was basically a restatement of the teaching of Jesus on love of neighbor. To pursue "the greatest happiness for the greatest number" is the equivalent of such love. But Mill's principle of utility is not grounded in some revealed truth; instead, he claimed it is a logical consequence of the natural human desire for happiness.

A Pig's Philosophy?

Mill followed Bentham in generally equating happiness with pleasure, but he introduced a qualitative distinction between pleasures which Bentham denied. The charge of "pig philosophy" had been leveled at Bentham's utilitarianism since Bentham had argued that all pleasures are equal, that "pushpin is as good as poetry" if it results in pleasure. All pleasure, as pleasure, is a good. Bentham's critics suggested that a pig happy in a mud puddle would be an ideal utilitarian. Mill, on the other hand, argued that qualitative distinctions between pleasures could and should be made. "It is better to be a human being dissatisfied than a pig satisfied." While a pig may have pleasures of mere sensation, human beings have the capacity for pleasures derived from imagination, feelings, and intellect. Who, then, is in position to decide which pleasures are preferable? Mill's response was that only a person who has experienced both pleasure X and pleasure Y was in position to judge which is preferable. He was convinced that the higher pleasures of human experience are qualitatively superior to mere animal sensations. This distinction ran into some philosophical difficulties for Mill, but such criticisms are beyond the intention of this book.

The Role of God

The role of belief in God is marginal, at best, in Mill's moral theory. He granted that belief in the supernatural may have once helped to support private and public morality, but he concluded that belief in God was no longer needed. Nor did he believe that belief in God was effective in producing moral persons. Furthermore, evidence or argument could not support belief in God. The argument from design for God's existence was interesting, Mill thought, but it gives us "no more than a probability" that God exists and gives us no information about the nature of such a God. Mill also believed that the general suffering of human beings and other creatures makes it impossible to believe that such a God can be both benevolent and all-powerful. He concluded that while one may believe in a benevolent God, this God must be severely limited in power. Human beings, by their ideals and actions, can help such a deity bring about more satisfactory conditions for human life. In that way, figures such as Jesus could serve as pictures of moral excellence. They could also aid in the establishing of a Religion of Humanity or a Religion of Duty.

While he believed there is no evidence for the immortality of the soul or for miracles, Mill granted that there are no arguments that stand strongly against such claims. Some basis for hope seemed to be important for Mill, and such beliefs tend to make room for hope. Religion, in this way, can have certain social utility. Mill generally avoided public comment on religious subjects. However, after his posthumously published *Three Essays on Religion*, Mill's non-religious admirers were disturbed because Mill did not totally discard religious aspirations and views. Meanwhile, Mill's religious critics claimed that his philosophy has resulted in intellectual bankruptcy and moral collapse.

An Egalitarian View

Even with a marginal role of God in Mill's philosophy, he still maintained an egalitarian perspective for a good and just society. There may be distinctions in the pleasures enjoyed by human beings, but Mill maintained that one person's happiness is never more important than another's. He agreed with Bentham's dictum: "Everybody to count for one, nobody for more than one." In Mill's words, the "ideal perfection of utilitarian morality" is "to do as one would be done by, and to love one's neighbor as oneself." In this claim, of course, lies the issue of just how one defines "neighbor." Mill would clearly apply that term to all of those who shared his English nationality and heritage. The challenge for Mill and for all egalitarian thinkers is whether this neighbor love can be demonstrated to members of other nations in competition or war with one's own. The question of just who belongs to my "tribe" remains. Nevertheless, in his description of a "religion of humanity," he hoped that the seemingly natural loyalty that persons have toward their nation and people could be extended to include all humanity.

The Fulfilled Life and Moral Obligation

John Stuart Mill's view of a truly fulfilled human life could not include some view of heaven after death since he was largely skeptical of matters religious. The major source of happiness, for Mill, was his dedication to a just and good society. His contributions to that end in England reflected his influence and accomplishments. He was clearly of an elite class of intellectuals in his day as a result of early and intense education and training at the hands of his father. Nevertheless, his view of a fulfilled life could be translated to the ordinary citizen by encouraging them to find fulfillment and happiness in living out their life in service of the larger community. Such service would be an expression of loving one's neighbor. His view of moral obligations to others could be summarized in his utilitarian motto: "The greatest good for the greatest number." This obligation would also be a reflection of his understanding of the precept to love the neighbor as oneself.

Of all the philosophers reviewed in this chapter, J. S. Mill comes closest to maintaining that traditional Christian moral principles can be sustained on non-religious grounds. His position, therefore, represents a challenge to a major claim of this book. An extended critique of Mill's utilitarianism will not be pursued here. He reflected much of the optimism of Enlightenment thinkers in his claim that if we all thoughtfully pursue our own self-interest then all who share life's journey with us will also benefit. This optimism came to be expressed in the thinking of Karl Marx, while a contrasting pessimism, of sorts, was developed by Friedrich Nietzsche. The views of these philosophers follow.

Karl Marx (1818–83)

"The philosophers have only *interpreted* the world differently; the point is, however, to *change* it." When Karl Marx made this observation, he was witness to the miserable social conditions resulting from an unregulated and rampant capitalist economic system. He was determined to change the world. Many of his ideas came from a variety of economists and philosophers. David Ricardo (1772–1825), reflecting the thoughts of John Locke (1632–1823) and Adam Smith (1723–90), argued that the value of any product is created by the labor put into the making of the product—the labor theory of value; Henri de Saint-Simon (1760–1825) had declared that history is shaped by conflicts between social classes; Georg W. F. Hegel

(1770–1831) had described the dialectical processes of history; and Ludwig Feuerbach (1804–72) revived philosophical materialism with its open atheism. Borrowing from these thinkers, Marx constructed a system of thought that, at one point in the twentieth century, was the official philosophy controlling nearly a third of the people on earth.

Marxian Materialisms

Marx adopted a thoroughly materialistic and deterministic view of both the physical and the social world. His materialism was ontological in that he believed that all reality, including human thought, is an expression of some form of matter. Nothing exists that is outside of or other than material entities. There is no God or transcended reality. Marx's "historical materialism" claimed that "the mode of production of the material means of existence" shapes the development and structure of any society. For example, a hunter-gatherer economic system will have a social structure quite different from that of a society with an agricultural base or one based on industrial production. He did not hold, however, to "ethical materialism" which maintains the material things of life are the good things to pursue.

Universal Determinism

Marx's determinism claimed that all events, natural and social, are caused by antecedent circumstances. The laws of chemistry and physics involve a mechanical determinism, while the forces of history and social life, though deterministic, are subtler and less open to precise predictions. With such explanations in place, religious ideas are no longer taken seriously but can be explained in terms of this materialistic determinism. The idea of God is a creation of human thought, he maintained, and played a role in the development of human history. As the "opiate of the people," religion is a means by which "oppressed creatures" seek to ease their pain. Marx also added that religion is the heart of a heartless world. However, when this pain is relieved through changes in the economic systems, such an opiate will no longer be necessary.

No Moral Advice Given

Marx did not set out to develop a moral philosophy that would inform persons about what is good and how to act rightly. Instead, he intended to explain how morality develops out of the economic structures of a society. As a scientist, Marx claimed to be purely descriptive, not prescriptive. He believed not only that morality is always linked to the wants and needs of human beings, but also that such wants and needs are shaped by the circumstances in which persons live. Fundamental to such circumstances is the economic system dominating that society. His aim was to describe the dynamics of history, especially in terms of the impact that economic systems had on any society. Moral systems, he believed, always reflect the economic systems in place at any time in history; therefore, an ideal moral system can develop only when people live in an economic system that frees them and enables them to be good. In contrast to the pessimism about human nature reflected in thinkers such as Hobbes, Marx optimistically believed that human nature is pliable and can be molded by changes in social and economic systems. Nurture is stronger than nature.

The Forces of Economic Systems

Marx argued that the prevailing economic system, at any stage of history, shaped the ideas, values, and moral convictions of those living at that time. In a capitalistic economic system, morality will reflect the competitive economic system and the "class struggle" between those who own the means of production and those who do the productive work. Given this analysis, Marx does not consider the capitalist who "exploits" labor to be morally blameworthy because the capitalist merely reflects the nature of the capitalist system. "Exploitation" was a technical term designed to *explain* the dynamics of the capitalist system, not a term to carry moral *judgment*. Nor would Marx fault labor organizations that could yield some power serving their own interests. The capitalist system necessitates such self-interested activities, and, consequently, those living under that system are not free to be good.

The Coming Classless Society

Marx believed that an ideal moral system can develop only when a just economic system is in place and the long historical struggle between classes has been overcome. This occurs when those who work on the means of production also own those means. The class system would then cease to exist. History, Marx believed, was moving inexorably toward such an ideal community. While the kingdom of heaven is no longer awaiting mankind, the kingdom of the classless society is promised. In this classless society, the long struggle between the classes will necessarily cease and bring peace and prosperity for all. In the meantime, all within the capitalistic system are members of either the owner or the working class. Some, like lawyers and physicians, have "class interests." Lawyers, for instance, seldom find their interests linked with the poorer working class. Marx believed that all persons—owners, workers, those with class interests—are motivated by self-interests and seek to work those out from within that economic system to the best that they are able. This is the dynamics of the class struggle.

The revolutionaries who understand the historical processes will, Marx believed, work toward the ultimate revolution that will bring in the classless society. Nevertheless, when the classless society arrives, the state would wither away since there would no longer be a need to defend class interests. The new human and economic relationships would make it possible for all to live out the motto: "To each according to their need; from each according to their abilities." The specifics of the moral relationships that would develop in that ideal society could not be predicted with precision. Scientific developments, for instance, could help shape moral patterns. The development of artificial means of birth control, for instance, could bring about changes in sexual moral patterns. Nevertheless, with the classless society in place, human relationships would reflect communal interests and the specifics of morality would develop naturally to meet the needs of the people. The dynamics of history have replaced the will of God.

Claiming to work as a scientist, Marx did not directly describe what he might believe to be a truly fulfilled human life—nor did he propose some theory of moral obligation. He clearly hoped for a coming society that would provide economic freedom and relative prosperity in a classless society. At that point in history, peoples and nations could live together in harmony and find ways of cooperation and caring that could meet the basic needs of life. Until that time arrived, Marx committed himself to understanding the economic dynamics of history and describing the processes that would lead to the classless society and the end of the class struggle.

Friedrich Nietzsche (1844–1900)

The son and grandson of Lutheran ministers, Friedrich Nietzsche became a passionate opponent to the Christian faith and its attendant morality. Although his last days were marked by mental illness, his writings bear the mark of a brilliant and searching mind. While capable of subtle arguments, much of the power of his writing stems from his use of striking aphorisms and metaphors. The major themes he pursued include the death of God and the consequent revaluation of values. He produced no formal system of philosophy, largely because he believed that all such systems build on self-evident truths that must, themselves, be challenged. He did not seek to be, as he put it, an "unriddler of the universe." However, if his aim was to provoke serious thought, he most certainly succeeded.

"God Is Dead"

Most widely known for his proclamation that "God is dead," Nietzsche regarded his pronouncement with misgivings as well as hope. If Darwin's theory of evolution and the implications of the collapse of religious faith came to be widely understood, Nietzsche believed that catastrophic wars could be part of the future. Much of his attention is given to the question of human values in a world where belief in God can no longer be taken seriously. With God no longer on the human horizon, "the sea, *our* sea, lies open before us. Perhaps there has never been so open a sea." In the following pages, I will briefly explore that "open sea" of values he posits and show how these values are related to the demise of God. Standard works on Nietzsche should be consulted for a more comprehensive view of this brilliant and disturbing philosopher.

The Will to Power

Central to Nietzsche's approach to values was his conviction that the "will to power" (German: *der Wille zur Macht*) exists as an elemental force in all of life. In human beings, this is an inner drive to express more than simply the will to live; it expresses the desire to affirm all human powers—physical, intellectual, emotional, psychical, and creative. The will to power was more than a mere struggle for existence. The will to power involves a will to war and a will to overpower others. Any attempt, then, to formulate some universal moral rule for all to follow is, for Nietzsche, a fundamental error that robs the human being of the vitality of life. Here Christianity and Judaism are major offenders since the Judeo-Christian ethic of love and compassion is so contrary to basic human nature that it produces only "botched and bungled lives." He had equal disdain for utilitarians, like Bentham and Mill, who believed that people are basically motivated by a desire for pleasure.

Slave and Master Moralities

Even the Christian ethic, Nietzsche claimed, expresses the will to power by developing a "slave morality" promoted by the weak in order to restrain the powerful who expressed a "master morality." In the master morality, "good" is the term of approval for those who are noble, those who directly express their will to power, those who are not ashamed to glorify themselves, and those who take pleasure in what is severe and difficult. Nietzsche would approve of the pleasure attendant to the feeling of increased power; but honest persons recognize that it is power they desire, not pleasure.

The contrasting slave morality arises from those who are weak and oppressed and who lack the courage of bold self-affirmation. In contrast to the values of master morality, slave morality exalts such qualities as sympathy, the warm heart, patience, humility, and friendliness. This is the morality of the "herd," those who fear the strong and the noble. This is the morality that springs from resentment and seeks revenge upon the strong by redefining the aristocratic virtues of power and pride as forms of evil. Nietzsche believed Christian morality subverts humanity. Nietzsche regarded Christianity as a seductive lie. It was a great piece of historical irony, he once remarked, that the Greek idea of "virtue," as the noble, powerful, and assertive man, became a term applied to the sexual purity of women.

The Fulfilling Life

In Nietzsche's thought, the connection between ontology and morality is clearly demonstrated. His boldly naturalistic worldview dismissed the idea

MORAL THEORIES AND WORLDVIEWS

of God; furthermore, he maintained that with the "death of God" the traditional moral values linked to belief in God must also collapse.[61]

Nietzsche's version of what would constitute a fulfilling life would appear to be an example of Kierkegaard's aesthetic stage, which was described in Chapter 3. The meaning of life is not to be found in religious faith nor in commitment to community moral values; rather, life's meaning is to be found in expressing the passionate vitality of life as joyous expressions of the various forms of human power. This life would include elements of the mood expressed in the Greek worship of Dionysus, who represented those vital aspects of life that acknowledge no restraints or boundaries—symbolized in the drunken frenzy of Dionysian worship.

On the other hand, however, Nietzsche maintained that there is another side of human nature that must also be honored—that of the cool and rational side symbolized by the God Apollo. The dark powers of the soul, symbolized by Dionysus, must be controlled and directed into creative acts of life through the use of Apollonian reason. However, in the end, this human life of flesh and blood is to be celebrated, not condemned and rejected in some display of humility and asceticism. For Nietzsche, the religious idea of "holiness" is merely a series of symptoms of an incurably corrupt body.

With the collapse of religious belief and traditional moral values, Nietzsche would deny that persons have any particular responsibility to be concerned about the fulfillment of others. His quest was for a life "beyond good and evil" that reflected higher values expressed in vitality and courage. Human beings vary, he held. The strong and vigorous pursue their power, while "herd men," like sheep, take refuge in conforming to the common trivialities of daily life. But the truly strong have no need to be bullies; they rejoice primarily in contests with others who are also strong. Neither the great athlete nor a great intellect finds joy in competing with a weak opponent.

For Nietzsche there are no external sanctions on the activities of the strong, no divine judge or judgment, and no problematic conscience. Yet the individual does have a price to pay, a sanction of sorts, in failing to pursue the "open sea" in the celebration of life that constitutes the higher morality. Failure to pursue this higher pathway brings with it the repression of the will to power resulting in the drudgery of conformity, debilitating weakness, resentment toward those who are noble and strong, and belief in a God who will finally reward and protect the weak and humble. Nietzsche was no lover of human beings as they are. He hoped that history would produce a higher kind of man, an *ubermensch* or "superman."

This higher man who has won his freedom disdains the comforts of Christians, women, and Englishmen.

Jean-Paul Sartre (1905–80)

While Søren Kierkegaard is often cited as the father of modern existentialism, the philosophical movement is most popularly linked to Jean-Paul Sartre. His novels and plays, perhaps more than his technical works, helped to move existentialism from the obscure recesses of academic philosophy to the broad cultural scene. More than a passing fad, existentialism, with its themes of anxiety, meaninglessness, and radical freedom, deeply influenced art, literature, psychology, and theology.

A Serious Atheist

Sartre took atheism seriously. He agreed with Nietzsche's pronouncement that "God is dead" and explored Dostoevsky's claim that "if God did not exist, everything would be permitted." With the demise of God, according to Sartre, we are left with the responsibility to invent or construct our own meanings and values. This is, he asserts, a "terrible freedom." Since there is no God who created a specific human nature or essence, the individual is left to define and create their own essence through free choices and projects. No divine realm exists that can reveal to us what should be and what we ought to do; nor can human reason discover or define a human nature or possible objective moral rules. Neither can there be a true science of humanity, since human freedom cannot be understood or contained within the causal structures that science attempts to discover. "Existence precedes essence" for human beings. We are what we make ourselves to be. Since no patterns exist for us to emulate or pursue, we are "condemned to be free" and must make those choices that define us as individuals. What Sartre describes is a human condition characterized by anguish, forlornness, loneliness, and a sense of abandonment. While Sartre repudiates religious theory as a basis for morality, he ends up by constructing a theory about human nature—that of a free being conscious of its freedom—to serve as the basis for his own perspective on morality.

Sartre on Morality

Sartre had no moral advice to give. He asserted only that we must choose and then bear the burden of our inevitably free choices. Such choices can never be justified in some objective way because no basis for justification exists. There are no divine laws revealed, no basic human nature to be found, and no "categorical imperative" to be discovered by human reason. For Sartre, any attempt to justify moral choices on the basis of some objective reality such as God or reason, constitutes a matter of self-deception—a lack of honesty about the human situation. In his more mature years, Sartre moved away from the severe individualism of his earlier works and recognized that individual freedom is curtailed by a capitalist system that exploits persons. While he came to accept aspects of a Marxist analysis of economic and social dynamics, he never accepted the ontological materialism and determinism of orthodox Marxism.

Authentic Existence

Instead of a concern about a fulfilling life, Sartre preferred to use the language of "authentic existence." Such existence would involve overcoming self-deception by recognizing our freedom and the burden of choice. The authentic person refuses to play a role or take on some kind of objective identity. The authentic person does not "play" at being a waiter, or clergyperson, or an existentialist philosopher. The inauthentic life is that of disguise, of playing roles, of excusing ourselves because of fate or circumstances. For the inauthentic person, image is everything.

Moral Responsibility

Regarding moral responsibility toward others, Sartre denied that such an objective responsibility could exist. While others are "mostly in our way," he was convinced that an honest and authentic human being would recognize the freedom of others. He, himself, chose to work in the French underground during the period of the Nazi occupation of France. However, his choice to be part of the resistance to the Nazis was his free choice; he did not claim that such action was morally required of others.

In terms of Kierkegaard's "stages," Sartre would reject both the moral and religious stages since neither have foundation and both would constitute a rejection of human freedom as well as being a form of self-deception. This leaves the aesthetic stage as Sartre's approach to the meaning of human life—assuming that Kierkegaard's three stages exhaust the options. The meaning of existence for the free individual, then, would consist of the full and honest recognition of freedom and the pursuit of those life projects by which we make ourselves into what we are. Finally, Sartre would advise us that human existence is absurd, and that the only meaning we can have is that which we affirm by pursuing our own commitments. Failing to live authentically as a free being, the individual faces the sanction of inauthenticity by living out life in some kind of "role" that denies their freedom. The self never becomes a self.

Summing Up

The central claim of this chapter has been that these philosopher's worldviews shaped their conclusions regarding the nature of a truly fulfilling life as well as possible implications of moral responsibility. This chapter is by no means exhaustive, and the descriptions often fail to do justice to the breadth and subtleties of the positions presented. Readers are encouraged to test this central claim as they explore other moral theories and as they reflect upon their own convictions about matters moral.

5

Religion-based Morality

> The religious perspective . . . is the conviction that the values one holds are grounded in the inherent structure of reality, that between the way one ought to live and the way things really are there is an unbreakable inner connection. What sacred symbols do for those to whom they are sacred is to formulate an image of the world's construction and a program for human conduct that are mere reflexes of one another.
>
> —Clifford Geertz[62]

The moral patterns of most cultures have, for good or ill, developed out of the religious traditions that shaped those cultures. In Western civilization, Judaism, Christianity, and Islam have been widely influential. All three are forms of ethical monotheism; hence, they are grounded in the conviction that God exists. Traditions in the Far East seldom reflect a clear parallel to Western monotheism; nevertheless, Hinduism, Buddhism, and Taoism each provide concepts that shape the moral patterns of their own distinct belief system. This chapter seeks to describe the major patterns of moral views rooted in various religions but will not attempt to justify or critique any of those represented.[63]

Religion-Morality Relationship

A preliminary question must first be raised: What possible relationships are there between religion and morality? Clearly, religion and morality have often been inescapably linked not only in the popular mind but also by persons of philosophical distinction. For instance, in the nineteenth century, the passionately religious Fyodor Dostoevsky asserted through a character in one of his novels that if God is dead, anything is permissible, and in the twentieth century the equally passionate atheist Jean-Paul Sartre believed that with the demise of God there is no longer any objective basis for morality. With no objective answers for our moral quest, Sartre concluded that we must freely choose with no hope for a rational justification of that choice. The influential seventeenth-century British empiricist, John Locke, believed that religious convictions were an important aspect of personal morality and that we have no good grounds for trusting an atheist. A century later, Immanuel Kant argued that a careful analysis of the very idea of morality leads one to *posit* the existence of God. On the other hand, some influential thinkers have maintained that moral traditions rooted in religious systems are irrational or morally corrupt in that such systems are often cruel, divisive, and vindictive.

At this point, three claims regarding the relationship between morality and religion will be made without any extended attempt to defend the claims. 1) There appears to be no direct correlation between atheism and immorality. In our culture, atheists and religious believers can and often do hold and practice the same general moral values. This is not an interesting philosophical point. Most of us, whether religious or not, absorb our moral values quite uncritically from our cultural setting. Hence, an atheist may hold rather traditional moral values even though these values are historically rooted in a religious worldview. 2) Systems of morality can be developed on purely naturalistic (non-religious) grounds. History is replete with such examples from Aristotle and Epicurus to contemporary thinkers. These moral beliefs, however, do differ in significant ways from morality grounded in religious beliefs. 3) The moral patterns of classical theistic traditions of the West cannot be rationally defended apart from the theological beliefs in which they are grounded.

Religion-Morality Distinction

Before describing some of the elements of religious morality as developed in various traditions, we must first recognize that being moral is not synonymous with being religious. It is true that all major religions include a moral pathway, yet these same religions serve their followers in ways that reach far beyond moral issues. These religious also provide believers with a basic set of concepts, symbols, and rites through which they come to understand not only the nature of the universe but also the meaning of their own personal venture through life. Religions deal not only with the question, "What ought I do?" they deal also with such questions as "Why am I here?" "Where am I going?" "What does it all mean?"

As the epigraph at the beginning of this chapter indicates, religions seek to be grand conceptual schemes that represent attempts to make sense out of the human venture as well as the cosmos in which persons find themselves. As religions attempt to explain the nature of things, their language is that of symbol, myth, and legend while their goal is to provide a way of walking through life with some sense of confidence, hope, and inner peace in a world too often full of pain and suffering. When a religion fails to bring this vision into place for believers, then they must look elsewhere for answers to these crucial questions.

Elements of Religious Worldviews

To understand a religion-based morality, the worldview in which it is grounded must be explored. All religious worldviews share two convictions about the human experience. First, they express an initial pessimism in that they believe that human life is broken, painful, and difficult. Many religious myths tell stories that account for that condition. The Buddha held that the first "noble truth" is simply this: "To live is to suffer." Religious language used to describe the human situation includes a variety of terms such as "lost," "fallen," "sinful," "blind," or "ignorant." Thus human beings find themselves in need of enlightenment, release, redemption, or salvation.

On the other hand, the major world religions also reflect an optimism which runs beyond that of most naturalistic philosophies. Every major living world religion teaches that, ultimately, there is a totally fulfilling answer to the problem of the human situation. Release (enlightenment, redemption, salvation) is possible. Such release always involves a moral dimension, but more than morality is involved. From the eye of religious belief, the moral pathway is always seen as fulfilling. Morality is not a burden to be tolerated; it is an integral part of the path toward the highest human fulfillment. To be sure, the moral pathway during life calls for courage and discipline in the face of suffering; yet, in the end, the promise of fulfillment is there. Most religions, in this sense, have a highly extended sense of delayed gratification. Heaven, for example, must wait until life's earthly journey is over.

Models of God's Role in Salvation Process

Since religions express a basic quest for salvation (Western monotheism), Nirvana (Buddhism), or release (Hinduism), an analysis of the role that "God"—or some alternative Reality—plays in such a quest would be fruitful. Views of the relationship between the salvation sought, the moral pathway to be traversed, and the activities of the Divine can be illustrated by three models.[64] Each model describes an interaction between mothers and their offspring. The mother represents the role of the Divine in the saving process while the child represents the human being in need of salvation. The major issue in each model is whether the child is saved through good works alone, by God's grace alone, or by a combination of good works and Divine grace. The terms "salvation" and "saved" are Western in mood but can be interchanged with the language of other traditions. The following descriptions explain the understanding of the "saving" process with no implied criticism of any particular model. However, major theological debates often grow out of differences among the models represented.[65]

Sea Turtle Model

The "sea turtle" model represents the view that salvation is achieved by "works alone." There is no Divine assistance involved. In nature, the sea turtle buries her eggs in the sand on the ocean beach and then returns to the sea completely ignoring her potential offspring. As the baby sea turtles hatch and make their way to the surface of the beach, they get no assistance from mother. Furthermore, they are often threatened by a variety of predators waiting for a meal of tender turtle. Instinctively, the baby turtle makes its way frantically to the safety (salvation, release) of the sea; but it is totally on its own since mother is not present to help or "grace" her child's journey. Hence, the model represents "salvation by works alone." In religious terms, the person is saved only by being obedient to the moral structures and religious duties such as the Law of Karma in Eastern religions. Western monotheisms have never reflected this model since they always subscribe to God's graciousness in some form. Most forms of Hinduism, Jainism, and early Buddhism do reflect this model; yet, in all these faiths, the moral pathway is always perceived as the fulfilling pathway.

Monkey-Hold Model

The second or "monkey-hold" model represents salvation through works in *cooperation* with grace. In this model, while the mother monkey (God) watches the child (the human person) at play on the jungle floor, she is aware of a leopard creeping toward her child. The child, itself, is initially unaware of the danger. The mother monkey leaps to the floor of the jungle, lifts the child and clasps it to her breast as she bounds to the safety of a tree. In this model, the initial action of the mother is crucial, but the cooperation of the child is also required for the child must cling to the mother to attain salvation. If the child fails to cooperate, it will fall again to the jungle floor and face destruction. Thus, salvation is initiated by a gracious act of God, but the believer must then cooperate with this gracious act by being obedient to the moral law as known. This second model represents the traditional Roman Catholic view of God's saving grace available through the church and the requirements of right belief and right moral actions on the part of the believer. The repentant sinner can be forgiven by God through the sacraments of the church, but the forgiven sinner always risks alienation from God through further sinful acts. Believers must exercise their part in the saving process through faithful obedience. Traditional Judaism and Islam reflect this model as well since both see the gift of the Divine Law (Torah, Sharia) as a gracious act of a compassionate God. Nevertheless, in both faiths the Law must be followed if salvation is to be achieved.[66]

Cat-Hold Model

The third or "cat-hold" model of salvation represents the position of "by grace alone." When mother cat (God) sees that her child is in danger, she picks it up by the nape of the neck and carries it off to safety. The kitten does nothing to contribute to the process, but merely curls up and trusts in the mother. This model represents Classical Protestantism where salvation is "by grace alone through faith." Neither good works nor correct beliefs contribute to the saving process. One "has faith" (trusts) only in God. This faith is, itself, seen as a gift from God—a position also held by the Roman Catholic Church. Of course one who truly trusts in God will also seek to live by the Divine will, but this obedience is not seen in any way as a *means* of being saved. Instead, having discovered and experienced the nature of God's saving love, the individual rejoices in that great gift and is transformed into a new creature. Believers do the will of God, not because they must, but because the will of God now reflects their own loves and desires. Furthermore, secure in their faith they trust that since they are elected—saved—by Divine grace, they will be eternally held in that grace. God will never abandon them.

Predestination

The logic of the third model led both Luther and Calvin—the two primary figures of the Protestant Reformation—to embrace predestination. In this they followed both Augustine and Aquinas. This doctrine asserts that only those whom God freely elects will attain Heaven and that no person can merit Heaven on the basis of their good works. It should be noted that this doctrine of predestination is not to be confused with a view often called fatalism or predeterminism. Both of the latter concepts hold that human choices cannot alter the future since all events are willed by God. "What will be, will be." Both Calvin and Luther, however, believed that our choices and actions can and do alter certain aspects of the future. The doctrine of predestination asserts only that human choices and actions cannot alter the believer's ultimate destiny, that of Heaven or Hell. While this cat-hold model reflects "Classical Protestantism," a variety of Protestant groups have taken a position more akin to the monkey-hold model.

Natural Law Theory

Since in all major religions the path of salvation (moksha, nirvana), always involves a moral dimension, religious traditions are necessarily concerned about properly discerning moral dimensions reflected in the will of the Divine. How does the believer come to know God's will or the rules of the proper moral pathway? One widely held position is the Natural Law Theory. This theory maintains that human reason can correctly discern proper moral rules and principles, in part, without the aid of Divine revelation. There are, according to this view, "natural laws" which exist in the natural world and can be discerned and understood by the human mind quite aside from revealed truth. (These "natural laws" have to do with moral truths, not "laws of nature" in the scientific sense.) The Roman Catholic view regarding artificial means of birth control grows out of this Natural Law tradition. The reasoning goes as follows: A rational examination of the phenomenon of sexuality in nature reveals that the primary purpose and end of sexuality is the procreation of children. Given this primary purpose within created nature, it follows that any act which deliberately frustrates this natural purpose is an immoral act. Since artificial means of birth control involve the thwarting of this natural scheme of things, the use of such means is an act against God's will as expressed in created nature.

Another example of natural truths of justice and morality in a different context is expressed in the Declaration of Independence. This document holds that there are "self-evident truths" such as "all men are created equal and are endowed by their creator with certain unalienable Rights, that among these are life, liberty, and the pursuit of happiness."

Moral Law As Revealed

Some religious traditions have held that human reason is unable, left to its own devices, to either understand the moral law or to live by it. Indeed, in their natural state of alienation from God, human beings are blind not only to the moral law but also to their own greatest good. So apart from the gracious saving work of God, including the revelation of the Divine will, human beings can neither know the moral law nor live by it. This position, of course, goes on to assert that God has, in fact, revealed the moral law to the human scene through some holy book and/or through some special persons. Conservative Protestants, Orthodox Jews, and Muslims reflect forms of this view. These groups hold that their scriptures—the *Bible*, the *Torah*, the *Qur'an*—are infallible by nature. Thus, to learn God's will, the believer turns to the holy book taken to be revealed by God (Yahweh, Allah). These traditions also involve learned commentaries on their scriptures that help in understanding and applying the Divine will. Less conservative groups within these traditions may not consider their scriptures to be wholly infallible since some parts of scripture may reflect old views of nature and science which we now know to be mistaken. Nevertheless, they believe that the central moral truths are to be found in the writings or in the history of the people recorded in the writings.

Moral Absolutists

An examination of religious ethics requires that a distinction be made between *Rule Absolutists* and *Principle Absolutists*. Both positions are absolutist since both hold that moral rules or principles exist that properly apply to *all* human beings in any time or place. Neither claims that all human beings know these rules or principles, nor do they claim that human beings follow these rules or principles even if they do know of them. They claim only that such absolute rules or principles exist and that human beings would benefit from knowing and obeying them.

Rule Absolutists

A Rule Absolutist would claim that the Divine moral Law consists of a series of specific rules which identify specific actions that one should perform as well as specific actions one should avoid. These rules are absolute in that they would correctly apply to any person at any time in any culture. Several of the traditional Ten Commandments—such as the prohibitions against stealing, killing, and adultery—would represent this position. According to some Rule Absolutists, lying is always wrong since it breaks a specific and absolute rule. Some Rule Absolutists would oppose all abortions, for instance, since they believe that abortion is the killing of an innocent human being.

Principle Absolutists

A Principle Absolutist, on the other hand, holds that there is one absolute general principle that properly applies to all persons at all times and in all places, while specific rules may not properly apply in all settings. This approach is reflected in what some refer to as "situation ethics." This view holds that the application of the one general moral principle has to be worked out within the context of a particular situation. Some Principle Absolutists, drawing on the teachings of Jesus and the writings of Saint Paul, hold that the one general moral principle is the Law of Love and that all basic morality is summed up in that Law. As Saint Paul wrote, "Love does no wrong to a neighbor, therefore love is the fulfilling of the law."[67]

This, of course, implies that one must decide just how to love someone in particular situations and under certain conditions since no specific actions are identified in the Law of Love. For instance, in some situations the loving act may involve the telling of a lie, while in another situation the loving act would involve the telling of truth. To use a common illustration: If you are concealing Jewish friends from the Nazis during World War II, should you tell the truth to the Nazi military police when they knock on your door and ask if you are hiding Jews on your premises? Would lying to the Nazis be morally wrong? A Principle Absolutist could argue that the ultimate moral principle is the Law of Love, and that one is therefore required to lie to the Nazis in order to honor that law. In that situation lying may be morally required. This setting is complex in its moral reach. If you are found to be lying to the Nazis, this could be disastrous to you, your family, and your Jewish friends. Working out just whom to love and how to love in that complex setting is rife with difficulties. While a Principle Absolutist might hold that there are times when one is morally required to lie, that Absolutist would probably agree that truth telling is a good general rule and a way to practice the Law of Love.

Some religious defenders of abortion rights use an argument parallel to the question of lying. They admit that while abortion could be a sad and difficult alternative, nevertheless there may be times when allowing an abortion is the loving thing to do in a given circumstance. If a woman's mental or physical health is at stake, or if she has been the victim of rape or incest, the loving thing to do in that situation may be to allow an abortion. Such an abortion would not be a loving act for the fetus, presumably, but the lives of others are also at stake. Few, if any, Principle Absolutists would see abortion used as a general means of birth control to be a legitimate expression of the Law of Love. I note, again, that neither the Rule Absolutist nor the Principle Absolutist necessarily believes that all people actually *know* of these rules or principles. Rather, they hold that people should *seek* to *know* and to *obey* them.

The Function of Divine Law

Another important distinction made in various formulations of religious ethics has to do with the function or purpose of the Divine Law. Four functions have been identified, though not all theologians would affirm the legitimacy of all four: 1) the saving function, 2) the civil function, 3) the normative function, and 4) the theological function.

Saving Function

The Divine Law exhibits the *saving function* when obedience to the Law becomes the *means* to salvation. The believer is saved or put in right relationship with God only by being obedient to the Law. Traditional Judaism and Islam hold this view of the Law, though both of these traditions have a strong sense of God's compassion and forgiveness. The Law of Karma or the moral law of cause and effect in traditions of the Far East represent much the same view. Classical Christianity has generally rejected this saving function of the Law in part because Christianity has a more pessimistic view of human nature expressed in the doctrines of the fall and original sin. The meaning of the crucifixion of Jesus in Classical Christianity also leads to the rejection of the saving function of the Law. Christians have generally held the view that human beings are sinners by their fallen nature and are self-centered and anxiety-driven. Furthermore, persons are not able to lift themselves by their own moral bootstraps, nor are they able to earn God's forgiveness and accepting love. Such forgiving love is, ultimately, a gift. To be sure, traditional Roman Catholicism and some Protestants have taught that if one is disobedient to the Divine Law, then one is in danger of being alienated from God and in danger of eternal rejection. Nevertheless, Catholicism has never taught that salvation can be attained only by being obedient to the Divine Law. Instead, one is saved through and by the grace of God conferred through the various sacraments of the church. Infant baptism, which removes original sin, exemplifies this initial act of saving grace without which, according to traditional Catholicism, the individual cannot be saved.

Civil Function

The *civil function* of the Law is exercised when the Law is used as a model for civil laws that are instituted by states or nations. Here, the Law is used to keep order and to seek to establish justice. Civil laws against murder represent such a use of the Law. These laws are used to restrain persons from doing evil deeds, not to provide a path to salvation. Nations or states seldom attempt to put all aspects of the Divine Law into forms of national or state laws, though some who think of themselves as theocracies approach this pattern.

Normative Function

The *normative function* of the Divine Law is expressed when this Law is taken as a basic guide for the living of one's life. Thus, while believers do not hold that they are saved or put right with God through obeying the Law, they nevertheless believe that a devout person accepts the Law as a moral guideline for life. Truth-telling would be one such guideline. Civil laws against lying are seldom made or enforced—except when under oath. (As if lying when not under oath is acceptable behavior?) In this normative function of the Law, the believer expresses loyalty to God and is part of the believer's quest for a fulfilling life journey.

Theological Function

The concept of the *theological function* of the Law is drawn largely from the writings of Saint Paul and is expressed in the Lutheran tradition. Here, the Law's main function is to show persons just how badly they err and how much they are in need of God's grace and help. The premise, here, is that no one is able to reach the high moral standards of, say, the Sermon on the Mount. To take that sermon seriously as a moral guideline would lead the believer to guilt and despair. The Law crushes human presumption and shows persons their need of grace. As Luther put it, God wounds in order to heal. This view of the Law holds that all persons stand guilty and condemned under the Law, and only by trust in the gracious love of God can one live without despair.[68] Nevertheless, these theologians continue, this discovery of the gracious love of God can change one's heart and turn one to a new direction in life. Now one lives, as far as one is able, by the Divine Law of Love. But one now lives by the Law, not in an attempt to earn God's love, but out of joyous response to the Divine Love that has already been freely bestowed. The well-known folk hymn "Amazing Grace" reflects the mood of this theological function of the Law.

Finally, a psychological analysis of human reactions to the Divine Law is offered by various religions as they address the question of why human beings seem to rebel against or fail to understand the very pathway that promises to lead to their joy and fulfillment. The answers offered by religious traditions usually involve some view of human ignorance, blindness, or willful rebellion.

The Buddha's Diagnosis: Ignorant Craving

Buddhism teaches that our basic problem is that of ignorance. After all, we start this life with nothing that can be called knowledge. Presumably, we learn as we grow older but learn by accepting, quite uncritically, what is told to us by our family, our culture, our peer group, or our gang. Consequently we *believe* that we know when we do not really *know* at all. We believe that what those around us value is really valuable; we believe that we know what is really good. The Buddha thought otherwise. He taught that we are victimized by "ignorant craving" which leads us to pursue things that are not truly desirable but bring us suffering instead. The evil deeds which people do—theft, murder, rape, war, violence—result from the ignorant craving of the perpetrators. The Buddha aimed to bring "enlightenment" so that his followers could, in properly understanding the nature of the human situation, overcome their ignorant craving and find the ultimate peace of Nirvana.

Augustine's Diagnosis: The Corrupt Heart

In the Christian tradition, Saint Augustine suggested a psychological explanation of human resistance to Divine Law. As he reflected on his days as a youth in North Africa, he thought of the night when he and some friends raided someone's garden, gleefully picked all the unripe pears off a tree and threw them to the pigs nearby.[69] As a man in his forties, he wondered why he and his friends *enjoyed* doing what they did that night. He concluded that they enjoyed doing it because they *knew* that it was wrong. For Augustine, then, evil was not a matter of ignorance. It is not that our *minds* fail us; the problem is that our *hearts* are corrupt. Evil is an expression of our fallen and sinful state: We love what we know we ought not to love, according to Augustine's analysis.

Autonomy–Heteronomy–Theonomy

Paul Tillich, a twentieth-century theologian, put the matter in a different way by analyzing the situation in terms of autonomy (self-law), heteronomy (other-law), and theonomy (Divine law).[70] Tillich held that we all desire to live by our own individual judgments of what is right and wrong. We want to be "autonomous." Furthermore, this desire is both normal and appropriate. For to be a genuine individual, to be authentic, we need to live by our own judgments, not those of someone else. Nevertheless, when we are confronted by the Divine Law in some form, we tend to experience such law as "over-against us." These laws appear to be "heteronomous," or laws that are "other" and not part of our own being. We experience these laws as irritating and inappropriate rules; we deeply resent them and may express this resentment through open or hidden rebellion. An analogous situation exists when youngsters come to the point of resenting the "laws" or rules laid down by parents and others. The youngster sees these laws as "other," as not part of their own choosing or being. This youthful rebellion is an example of the "rebellion of autonomy against heteronomy." Finally, Tillich suggests that religious believers come to see that the Divine Law that first appeared to be foreign or *other* is, in reality, an expression of their own essential being and not against them at all. This, then, is the state of "theonomy," whereby believers come to realize that the Divine Law is truly an expression of their own essential nature and is, therefore, a means of being truly fulfilled.

This chapter has attempted to describe some of the major facets of morality rooted in religious belief systems. These descriptions have, of course, been brief and have not expressed some of the fine nuances of these traditions. Furthermore, this chapter has been purely *descriptive*. No attempt was made to defend the truth of any of the positions or to criticize them. It would appear that they cannot all be true since they often hold contradictory positions. It may be that all of them are, in fact, false. On the other hand, perhaps one of them is close to the truth.

6

Self, Others, and Rights

Man . . . is simply the most formidable of all beasts of prey, and, indeed, the only one that preys systematically on its own species.

—William James[71]

Then conquer we must, when our cause it is just; and this be our Motto—"In God is our Trust."

—Frances Scott Key

If you love those who love you, what reward have you? Do not even the tax collectors do the same?

—Matthew 5:46

All moral theories, I have maintained, must deal with two basic issues: 1) What constitutes a truly fulfilling life? 2) Do persons seeking their own fulfillment have any obligation to help others do the same? The first issue was explored in chapter 3. This chapter will examine the concept of obligation. Three distinct issues will be analyzed: 1) What contributions do others make, positively or negatively, to my own quest for fulfillment? 2) Do I have any obligation to aid others in their quest for fulfillment as I pursue my own? 3) Do certain human rights exist which imply that persons have obligations toward others?

Regarding the first issue, it is clear that we are linked to others in various ways as we seek fulfillment. Some links are not important since the persons involved touch our lives only marginally. On the other hand, some relationships are so intimate and rich that our own flourishing is inescapably tied to them. Family and loved ones almost always constitute a crucial aspect of any life quest. To the degree that my spouse and children flourish, I also tend to flourish. Hence, the quest for fulfillment is rarely a *selfish* pursuit, though our own *self-interests* may be involved. Properly defined, "selfish" actions are those pursued solely for one's own self-interest without any concern for the interests of others. The aid I give to my child while nourishing her through an illness would not be selfish since I have positive interest in my child's survival. On the other hand, interests in my child's good fortune is certainly self-referential since my child's flourishing will often contribute to my own.

As our life connections to others become distant and less intimate, our active interest in their well-being tends to diminish. The influential nineteenth-century British philosopher, Henry Sidgwick proposed:

> We should all agree that each of us is bound to show kindness to his parents and spouse and children, and to other kinsman in a less degree; and to those who have rendered services to him, and others whom he may have admitted to his intimacy and called friends; and to neighbors and to fellow countrymen more than others, and perhaps we may say to those of our own race more than to black or yellow men, and generally to human beings in proportion to their affinity to ourselves.[72]

In this analysis, Sidgwick echoes David Hume's observation that the most we can hope for in human relationships is a "confined generosity." A number of contemporary philosophers also reflect Sidgwick's view by suggesting that human beings work out their life commitments in ever-widening circles of identification.[73] The implication is that the human scene is deeply marked by "tribal" relationships of various kinds.

Sidgwick's observations underline two fundamental issues. First, it is clear that our own flourishing is linked closely to persons with whom we have affinity. These circles of affinity or identification usually begin with family, but may expand to clan, club, gang, community, ethnic group, social rank, nation, or religious community. All these factors reflect how we identify those who are "our own" or "our kind of people." Furthermore, in making those distinctions, we also identify those who are not "our own" or "not our kind of people." In just this way we tend to divide the world into "us" and "them," and classify not only those who contribute to our flourishing but also those who may stand in our way. As we pursue our interests as well as our self-referential interests, those distinctions inevitably become part of our life commitments and plans.

Obligations to Others

The second issue underlined by Sidgwick's observation is how these natural circles of affinity are related to the concept of moral responsibility. The question, here, is that of the appropriate and rational goal for human actions. Is it rational for an individual to pursue only their own self-interest, including self-referential ones? Or is it rational, at least at times, to pursue the interests of others at some cost to one's own? A central teaching in the Biblical traditions would suggest that persons have deep responsibilities regarding the welfare of others: "You shall love your neighbor as yourself" is first found in Leviticus 19:18 and is caught up in the teachings of Jesus in all three of the synoptic Gospels—Matthew, Mark, and Luke. This theme will be explored later in this chapter.

Henry Sidgwick, in wrestling with the tensions between self-interest and obligation to others, did not find a way to adjudicate between rational egoism and utilitarianism, two highly influential but conflicting moral theories. He called this conflict the "Dualism of Practical Reason." Echoing the ancient Greeks, Sidgwick argued that rational egoism—the fundamental and rational aim of every person is that of their own interests—was a self-evident principle. However, he also concluded that utilitarianism—the greatest good for the greatest number—is also self-evident. Sidgwick found no way to reconcile this apparent conflict between self-interest and moral duty that has long existed as a basic issue in moral philosophy. Indeed, it is just the conflict that creates much philosophical reflection.

Rational Egoism as Primary Principle

In contrast to Sidgwick, I take the position that the primary self-evident principle is that of rational egoism and that the utilitarian position, as formulated by Bentham and Mill, falls back on a form of rational egoism for its justification. This is consistent with my assertion that all classic moral theories promise fulfillment for the person walking the moral pathway as defined by a particular theory. Morality, finally, is *for* us. My defense of this approach will be more fully developed in chapter 7 where the question "Why be moral?" will be addressed. To blunt initial criticism of rational egoism as a first principle, I note that rational egoism is not selfishness. This is true since our own interests are often positively linked to the self-interest of others. Furthermore, the founder of utilitarianism, Jeremy Bentham, embraced *psychological egoism*, the descriptive theory that people always and *necessarily* act to satisfy what they perceive to be their best interests.

> Nature has placed mankind under the governance of two sovereign masters, pain and pleasure. It is for them alone to point out what we ought to do, as well as to determine what we shall do.[74]

While modifying certain aspects of Bentham's position, John Stuart Mill retained this psychological egoism. Indeed, both taught that various sanctions teach us that our own quest for happiness requires us to become good utilitarians. Such an argument implies that rational egoism is the primary principle and that utilitarianism is derivative. The point that both Bentham and Mill seek to make is that our own happiness, which we necessarily seek as rational creatures, is inescapably linked to the happiness of others. At one level such a claim seems to be intuitively or even empirically true; but on another level it raises the question of whether or not our own happiness is tied to the happiness of *all* others, or just those with whom we have the strongest affinity or identification. The question of whether or not our natural tribalism can be overcome is still with us.

Roots of Tribalism

In a broad sense, affinity to others is linked to traditions in which we are often rooted. Sociologist Robert Bellah asserts:

> Our lives make sense in a thousand ways, most of which we are unaware of, because of traditions that are centuries, if not millennia old. It is these traditions that help us to know that it does make a difference who we are and how we treat one another.[75]

Philosopher Alasdair MacIntyre makes a similar point by showing that our stories are basic in establishing our connections with others.

> Man is in his actions and practice, as well as in his fictions, essentially a story-telling animal. . . . I can only answer the question "What am I to do?" if I can answer the prior question, "Of what story or stories do I find myself a part?" . . . Deprive children of stories and you leave them unscripted, anxious stutterers in their actions as in their words. Hence there is no way to give us an

> understanding of any society, including our own, except through the stock of stories which constitute its initial dramatic resources.[76]

These stories help us understand who we are by showing us the group to which we belong. But what constitutes belonging to a group? How is it that we establish a position that makes a distinction between *us* and *them*? Or, as Ninian Smart phrased it: What constitutes "ushood"? One of the most powerful boundaries that shape ushood is that of national identity. A nation is a whole of which citizens are a part.

> Its citizens are woven together by the strong threads of rituals— the very speaking of the same language, . . . the shape of values imparted through education, the more explicit rites of the nation through its anthem and flag, the sense of belonging and pride celebrated through football matches and Olympiads, the solemn demands of war, the remembrance of the sufferings of the past and their sad but glory-giving celebration, the feel for the ancestors, the general willingness to join one's country's armed forces, the expectation that to die for one's nation is a great and glorious thing. Such consciousness is acknowledgement of a particular and solemn ushood, in which we individuals merge together in solidarity, and are conscious of the nation both as something which is out there and as something in which each one of us participates.[77]

In much of the modern world, as Smart notes, the nation is the ultimate group which generates not only solidarity but also the duties of self-sacrifice. National identity is, in the modern world, the most common and powerful form of tribalism that is expressed in the command to kill as a basic duty. Smart places special emphasis on the matter of killing.

> Warfare itself is one of the great sacraments of mankind. Warfare is much more than killing or being killed; it transforms men, baptizes them with fire, leads them to the highest sacrifice, gives the nation a sense of its own destiny. It aims at victory, and the aggrandize-ment of national substance. . . . But, above all, in causing and suffering death, warfare feeds the national glory.[78]

Ancient documents and histories reflect Smart's analysis of warfare in their descriptions and celebrations of various wars. The *Iliad* and the *Odyssey*, epic Greek poems, describe the Trojan War, a conflict between the Greeks and the city of Troy. According to these epics, the war was fought almost 1200 years before the Common Era. The Hebrew Bible, the Christian Old Testament, recounts a number of battles between the tribes of Israel and other tribes in Canaan in the thirteenth century BCE. The stories are a mix of legend and revised history, according to Biblical scholars, but they do function as celebrations of a victorious people. Commonly dated to the second century BCE, the Hindu classic, the *Bhagavad Gita* (The Song of God), recounts a dialogue between prince Arjuna and his charioteer, Krishna, as they anticipate a *righteous* war. More recent accounts of war set to music would include "La Marseillaise" and "The Star Spangled Banner," national anthems of France and the United States. The bloody lyrics of the French national anthem illustrate Smart's description of the significance of warfare.

A nation, itself, is constituted by many factors where *territory* is basic. A people without a land of their own cannot become a nation since it fails to have a territory that grants not only a symbolic significance but also something like sacred space. The Zionist movement is an example of the significance of a land for a people. In its early days, the Zionist movement was driven more by the need to return to a land rather than by deep religious convictions. As the nation of Israel began to take form, the influence of Fundamentalists within Judaism—the Gush Emunim—linked the land to the belief that God had granted the land to the Jews. The Palestinians reflected a similar dynamic in that they believed the land was rightly theirs and that Muslim ethics calls on the faithful to defend their land as well as their faith. The tragic struggle between the Palestinians and the Zionists involves both claims on the legitimacy of a territory and religious beliefs.

The Palestinian/Israeli struggle reflects other factors that often define a nation: language, religion, and biological descent. For many nations, those three factors are shared by the vast majority of the population, as in Italy where the national language is Italian, and where Roman Catholicism is the religious identity—perhaps even for those who profess no faith of their own. In the Far East, the Japanese for centuries found their national identify linked to their language, their biological heritage, Shinto religion, and to their islands—the origins of which are recounted in the Shinto myths.

The challenge the United States faced—and still faces—is that of building a sense of national identity among immigrants who represent a variety of languages, religions, and biological descent. No doubt the dominant Christian background, the English language, European heritage, the developing territories and states, and the rituals of flag and nation all contributed to the early sense of being an "American." The factor of "whiteness" that is linked—in not too subtle ways—to this identity has been a major challenge to liberal and democratic proclamations.

Church and State Separation

The constitutional separation of church and state was, perhaps, never solved theologically; nevertheless, this principle established a practical sense of tolerance and enabled citizens to feel like loyal Americans even if their religious beliefs were different or absent altogether. The church-state separation also largely eliminated the need to choose between loyalty to one's religious faith or to the nation. At times, of course, specific religious beliefs are overruled by the courts if, for instance, they appeared to endanger the life or welfare of a child. Nevertheless, the believers were not forced to choose between faith and nation since they remained citizens even though their practices ran afoul of the law. It is possible, evidently, to "give unto Caesar that which is Caesar's and unto God that which is God's." Seldom in the modern world is there a forced choice between religious belief and national loyalty; therefore, it is difficult to ascertain which of the two might make the ultimate claim for a believer's loyalty.

The dichotomy between "us" and "them" can be traced in terms of national identity, biological and racial connections, language, territory, social status, and religious beliefs. All these create in-groups and out-groups. This dichotomy, as history demonstrates, also prescribes just whom we will care about first and foremost. It appears that it is "natural" for us to support the quest for fulfillment of those with whom we find some affinity. Indeed, evolutionary processes may well have wired our genes for just this sort of natural affinity. On the other hand, it also seems natural for us to ignore or undercut the attempts of others who seek fulfillment if their quest conflicts with our self-interests or the interests of those we cherish. We may claim to love our neighbor, but we still ask, "Who is my neighbor?" As Emerson once said, "do not tell me, as a good man did today, of my obligation to put all poor men in good situations. Are they *my* poor?"[79]

Religious Belief and Tribalism

Can religious beliefs shape in-group and out-group boundaries in significant ways? Any attempt to answer this question is riddled with complications. Current books explore the role religion plays in violent eruptions around the earth and lead to the clear conclusion that religion, as powerful human belief systems, can be used by evil people for evil purposes.[80] Modern technology suffers the same fate. On the other hand, there are

SELF, OTHERS, AND RIGHTS

examples of movements for justice and fairness that are grounded in religious convictions.

The issue is also complicated by the question of causal relationships between the belief espoused and the good or evil actions that appear to be linked to those beliefs. Do religious beliefs *cause* persons to do evil deeds? Or do those who have evil intentions choose to use religious justifications? Conversely, do religious beliefs *cause* persons to do good deeds? Or do persons who are disposed to be good use religious beliefs to support their good deeds? The difficult question is whether religious belief, by its nature, is basically a force for the general good of humanity or whether it is largely an expression of tribalism that generates divisions and conflict. Empirical data, alone, seems not to provide conclusive evidence for a definitive answer.

That believers can be powerfully bonded together by shared religious convictions seems beyond doubt and is reflected in scriptures and traditions. The *shema* (hear) in Deuteronomy 6:4–9 declares the unity and commitment of the people of Israel that follows from their status as a people chosen by Yahweh. In shaping the Christian tradition, Saint Paul wrote, "There is neither Jew nor Greek, there is neither slave nor free, there is neither male nor female, for you are all one in Christ."[81] In one of his last sermons, Muhammad declared that all Muslims should know that all other Muslims are their brothers. The vow of Buddhist monks reflects the same sense of affinity: "I take refuge in the Buddha, in the Dharma [foundation doctrines], and in the Sangha [the monastic order]." Traditional Shinto religion in Japan reflected perhaps the most potent expression of the unity of a people through the Shinto myths. These myths tell not only that the islands of Japan have divine origin, but also that the Japanese peoples themselves are descendants of the *kami* (spirits, deities, gods). All these declarations and symbols of affinity clearly designate in-group status in these various traditions. The question remains as to whether or not religious traditions have ways of overcoming parochial identities and are able to relate in supporting ways to peoples of other traditions.

Love of Neighbor

Rooted in the Biblical traditions, the admonition to "love your neighbor as yourself" would appear to lead the believer beyond parochial identity to a wider circle of concern. However, the early formulation of the admonition in the book of Leviticus reflects an in-group identity:

> You shall not hate in your heart anyone of your kin; you shall reprove your neighbor, or you will incur guilt yourself. You shall not take vengeance or bear a grudge against any of your people, but you shall love your neighbor as yourself.[82]

The following footnote regarding the above passage clarifies the use of several terms: "your kin," "neighbor," and "any of your people.":

> *Neighbor* here means a fellow Israelite . . . however, the law to love your neighbor as yourself is extended to include the resident alien (vv. 33–34).

The question of "Who is my neighbor?" is raised in all three of the synoptic Gospels. In Luke's account, Jesus responds to the question with the Parable of the Good Samaritan. The Christian tradition generally takes Jesus's response to mean that *neighbor* includes all human beings. Nevertheless, Christians have struggled with the command to love the neighbor when the neighbor—as nation or individual—runs into conflict with the interests of said Christians. Loving everyone is a high bar to acknowledge in a world where human beings reflect the description given by William James in the epigraph to this chapter: "Man . . . is simply the most formidable of all beasts of prey, and indeed, the only one that preys systematically on its own kind."

The Quakers can be cited as a religious belief system that minimizes or essentially removes in-group status. At one level, Quakers and primitive headhunters share a basic moral rule: One ought not take the head of someone from your own tribe. The significant difference between these two groups is the definition of "tribe." Tribal boundaries are reasonably clear to the headhunter. If you want a head, you go outside of your tribe to harvest it from enemies. The Quakers, on the other hand, have an expansive view of "tribe" since they believe that their tribe encompasses all humanity. Hence, you cannot harvest a head from anyone, for no one is outside of your tribe. Classical Quaker pacifism reflects the conviction that all human beings belong to the in-group. This conviction of inclusiveness is rooted in the Christian tradition that nurtured George Fox, founder of the Society of Friends, and his early followers.[83] As part of the left wing of the Protestant Reformation, Fox put forward the doctrine of the "inner light" drawn from the Gospel of John 1:9. Arguing that the "light of Christ" is available to all, even those who have not heard the preaching of the gospel, Fox held that this light is present as a seed in all persons and can be nurtured so that the Spirit of Christ dwells fully within the heart. Out of this foundation, the Quakers have long demonstrated social concerns reflected in people like Robert Owen, John Woolman, and William Penn. They were, for instance, early and powerful opponents of slavery. The Quakers are best known for their consistent pacifism that is rooted in the doctrine of the "inner light."

> It is not lawful for Christians to resist evil or to fight in any cause ... [war is] as opposite to the Spirit and doctrine of Christ as light to darkness. . . . Strange that men made after the image of God should bear the image of roaring lions; tearing tigers, devouring wolves, raging boars.[84]

The Quaker position is summarized here as one example of how religious belief can provide a foundation for a socially conscious and care-oriented attitude toward *all* persons. However, the example of the Quakers is not to be construed, here, as an argument designed to show that the Quaker position represents genuine Christianity or that the Quaker position is either rational or justified in some other way. These questions are left open in this discussion.

Some religions of the Far East have ameliorated tensions between groups and established a more universal sense of identity through the principle of non-injury (*ahimsa*). In its most fully developed form in Jainism, *ahimsa* requires the deeply spiritual ascetics to avoid injuring any living entity—including the lice on their bedding. Jains practice non-injury as a means of achieving their own fulfillment since injuring a living creature is believed to be an act that creates bad karma and impedes liberation from the cycle of rebirths. In Hinduism and Buddhism the principle is honored but not as strictly observed. *Ahimsa* was adapted to the nonviolent social and political movements of Mohandas Gandhi and Dr. Martin Luther King Jr. Gandhi's nonviolent approach to the British grew out of Jain and Hindu teachings as well as the influence of Christian Quakers he had met in South Africa. In order to square his nonviolence principle with the *Bhagavad-Gita*, a Hindu spiritual classic, Gandhi chose to interpret the violent passages in that work as allegorical. Dr. Martin Luther King Jr. was influenced by Gandhi as well as his own Christian tradition as he helped shape the civil rights movement. Both Gandhi and King represent leaders whose religious beliefs enabled them to escape narrow tribalism and move toward an inclusive view of justice and social policy.

The historical examples above demonstrate that religious beliefs not only bond a community of believers together but can also, at times, develop an inclusive identity with all human beings. However, history is also replete with examples that demonstrate the divisive and tragic results of religious belief. While other factors were often involved, the list of historical conflicts that included powerful religious dimensions would include the Crusades of the Middle Ages with the Christian battle cry of *Deus Volt* (God wills it), the spread of Muslim armies across North Africa and into Spain and France, and the variety of conflicts resulting from the Reformation.

Representatives of radical religious groups that have supported terrorism include Reverend Paul Hill, the Christian pastor and convicted anti-abortion killer; Dr. Baruch Goldstein, the Jewish physician who gunned down more than thirty Muslims during their morning prayers; Osama bin Laden, the Muslim alleged to have bankrolled terrorist acts including the 9/11 destruction of the Twin Towers in New York City; and Simranjit Singh Mann, a Sikh political leader suspected of masterminding the assassination of Indira Gandhi.[85] The history of the Mormons provide an example of how a charismatic leader and a claim to revealed and absolute truth can lead true believers to acts of horrific violence.[86]

In spite of certain evidence that belief in God has helped to create peace and justice among peoples, can religion in general be defended in the light of the bloody history involving various faiths? Defenders of religion might suggest that the Nazi and Communist movements, both enemies of religion, produced tragedies of immense proportions. However, those examples show only that evil can be perpetrated from a variety of ideologies; they do not excuse the evil done in the name of God. The jury is still out on this issue and a variety of voices hold court. A closing note on this issue comes from a scholar who has studied religiously motivated violence and nevertheless holds a hopeful view regarding religion's role in the human enterprise.

> Religion gives spirit to the public life and provides a beacon for moral order. At the same time it needs the temper of rationality and fair play that Enlightenment values give to civil society. Thus religious violence cannot end until some accommodation can be forged between the two—some assertion of moderation in religion's passion, and some acknowledgment of religion in elevating the spiritual and moral values of public life. In a curious way, then, the cure for religious violence may ultimately be in a renewed appreciation of religion itself.[87]

Human Rights

Having explored the first two issues raised in this chapter, the question of human rights must be examined. In claiming that persons have a right of any kind, two assertions are being made. First, a person is entitled to behave in a certain way under certain circumstances. If free speech is a right, then persons have a right to express their views or opinions—under certain circumstances. Second, persons should have certain expectations about the behavior of other persons in their relationships with persons who have a particular right. Thus, if a person has a right to life, this right would restrict any attempt by another to take the life of the person with that right. These two assertions suggest that claims about rights have to do with what a person may be allowed to do and what constraints may be placed upon the actions directed at another person. Rights, in this way, reflect both freedom and restraint.

Among many complex issues raised by the question of human rights are the following: 1) Are there such things as *human rights*, and what might they be? 2) Are human rights *discovered* as part of what might be called the nature of things; or are human rights *invented* as a means of dealing with moral and political issues? 3) How is a claim about human rights to be justified? 4) If human rights exist, do these rights imply obligations on the part of others? 5) What types of sanctions are appropriate if someone (or some group) fails to honor certain obligations imposed on that person (or group) by the existence of certain rights? 6) How does the idea of God (or some correlate) inform certain claims about human rights, and can such claims be sustained in the absence of belief in God? While a detailed examination of the concepts of rights, liberties, and duties cannot be accomplished in this work, some distinctions regarding language about rights would be helpful at this point. After these distinctions are made, the question of the existence of human rights and their possible justification will be pursued.

Legal rights exist and have an adequate grounding in the actions of an appropriate governing body. The first ten amendments to the Constitution of the United States, commonly known as the Bill of Rights, are examples of legal rights. While such legal rights are generated by the actions of some governing authority, some persons believe that such rights are, themselves, grounded in objective and universal moral principles. On the other hand, others believe that legal rights exist just because a governing authority has declared such rights. Further grounding or justification is neither needed nor available.

Civil rights are a special case of legal rights that deal largely with matters of justice and fairness. *Natural rights*—if such exist—are independent of the actions of any specific governing body or legal entity but are, instead, human rights which exist in the very nature of things. They are often thought of as being rooted in some metaphysical or religious reality. Thomas Jefferson (1743–1826) included "life, liberty, and the pursuit of happiness" as examples of such natural rights. The task of government, for Jefferson, was not to invent or formulate such rights but to "secure them" by forming legal structures that would protect such rights.

A different view of natural rights is found in the works of Thomas Hobbes (1588–1679) who held that in the "state of nature," where no civil authority or governing body exists, all people would have a "right of nature" to "do what he would, and against whom he thought fit, and to possess, use and enjoy all that he would, or could get."[88] For Hobbes, to "have a right" in that setting is equivalent to "having the power." In this sense, the lion has the "right of nature" to kill and eat what it can. For Hobbes, this right of nature has no moral implications whatsoever.

Human rights—if these exist—are important rights generally considered to be universal in that they apply to all human beings. As *inalienable*, such rights cannot be given away by a person holding them nor can they be taken away by others. The assertion of human rights has appeared conspicuously at the two points of history, one being in the Declaration of Independence made by the Second Continental Congress on July 4, 1776. The language of that declaration contains clear religious affirmations in appealing to the "Laws of nature and of Nature's God." This religious affirmation is included in the famous lines from the Declaration of Independence (July 4, 1776): "We hold these Truths to be self-evident, that all Men are created equal, that they are endowed by their creator with certain unalienable Rights, that among these are Life, Liberty, and the pursuit of Happiness."

Another significant claim about human rights appeared in 1948 with the Universal Declaration of Human Rights formulated by the United Nations. This document differs in a significant way from the Declaration of Independence in that it avoids specific religious grounding for such rights. Instead, in Article 1, it makes a number of assertions which stand without any attempt at justification: "All human beings are born free and equal in dignity and rights. They are endowed with reason and conscience and should act toward one another in a spirit of brotherhood."[89] The authors of this Declaration of Human Rights either believed that such claims are sufficiently self-evident, or they deliberately chose to avoid any philosophical or religious defense of such assertions. Agreement on the claims themselves was easier to achieve than an agreement on the justification for such claims. The aim of this 1948 Declaration is expressed in the words of the Preamble as "a common standard of achievement for all peoples." These rights serve as goals to be pursued as well as a basis for protest and for policy reform. Not all philosophers would view such rights as self-evident and would call for some type of justification of these claims. Nevertheless, this Universal Declaration has been widely honored in word if not in deed.

The shift from the use of religious language to justify claims about human rights in the Declaration of Independence in 1776 to the absence of any justification at all in the 1948 Universal Declaration illustrates the question at hand. This question can be formulated in two ways: 1) Can we *know* that human rights exist? 2) How can claims about human rights be justified? In keeping with the general intent of this work, no attempt will be made to provide any justification of human rights claims. Instead, some of the major options that have been proposed by philosophers will be explored. The following list should not be considered exhaustive; rather, these examples suggest certain ways of responding to the question.

The idea of human rights comes on the scene comparatively late in our history. Indeed, it appears that Thomas Paine was the first to use the specific expression "human rights" in his *Rights of Man*, published in 1791.[90] Long before rights language was formulated, the focus had been on the concept of duty. Duty, in turn, was related to the idea of some type of universal laws (God or nature) which set forth the duties required of persons. As Gandhi observed in the twentieth century, "The true source of right is duty."[91]

One attempt, then, to justify the claim that human rights exist is to ground the claim in some religious belief. This approach, of course, could be judged as successful only if the religious claims themselves can be justified—an issue I leave as an open question. In this justification of human rights, the religious belief would include the concept of duty linked to laws understood as given by God. Later, the concept of rights would be developed as a logical concomitant of those duties. One argument would go something like this: If God commands that I ought not kill my neighbor Y, then I have a duty not to kill Y. But if I have a duty not to kill Y, then it follows that Y has a right to life that I must honor.

Human Rights and Natural Law

Another approach to justifying the claim that human rights exist involves an appeal to natural law. Historically, this appeal was almost always linked to some idea of God or a divine reality that brought such laws into being or sustained and enforced them. This appeal to natural law is another way of grounding rights in a religious belief system. The first-century BCE Stoics were the first to speak of natural laws as a set of essential, eternal laws required for the happiness of individuals and for social harmony. For these Stoics, the entire universe was governed by the laws of a rational God. Physical laws governed the movements of objects, while moral laws expressed the right actions to be undertaken by human beings. These laws can be discovered because individuals have within them a divine spark or rational seed. Furthermore, these laws were understood to be universal and objective, applying appropriately to all human beings at every time or place.

Thomas Aquinas (1225-74) adapted both Stoic thought and that of Aristotle in formulating his own view of natural law. Key elements in his natural law theory included several claims: 1) God created human beings with a rational nature that enables them to discover those laws that help them to live and flourish in ways appropriate to human nature; 2) These laws can be known by reason, without revelation or knowledge of God; 3) Since these laws are unchangeable and universal, they should be used by all human communities to evaluate the laws of their societies; 4) Civil laws which are not in line with natural laws lose their status as true laws. Applying this natural law approach, for instance, Aquinas held that it is natural for persons to desire to sustain and continue their lives; therefore, one is obliged to protect life and health and to avoid suicide and carelessness.

John Locke (1632-1704) reflected the natural law tradition in his convictions that, by the use of reason, human beings could discover the moral rules that conform to God's laws. Furthermore, this divine law was to be seen as "the only sure touchstone of moral rectitude." Locke extended this concept of natural law by claiming that there are natural rights that represent the other side of the duties entailed by natural law. If there is, for instance, a natural law and a duty to preserve life, then a human being has a "right to life." This type of argument led Locke to affirm that three fundamental rights exist—the right to life, liberty, and property. A century later, Thomas Jefferson drew upon John Locke's views when he penned the Declaration of Independence with its claim that "all men are endowed by their creator with certain unalienable Rights." For the third right, Jefferson substituted "the pursuit of happiness" for Locke's "property."

Another attempt to justify the claim to human rights grows out of the conviction that each human being has some special status as a person who must be honored. This view is often linked to a religious justification of rights through the claim that the creative act of God endows each person with a basic sacredness. Some argue that the claim of the "sacredness of personality" or the "infinite worth" or the "dignity" of a human being requires a link to a religious claim of some kind.[92]

On the other hand, some maintain that the claim of a special status for persons need not be rooted in a religious claim as such. For instance, some in the human rights field hold that the concept of human dignity itself is the ultimate justification for human rights.[93] So when the question is raised about why one should respect human rights, the response would be that human dignity is violated if such rights are not respected. While this argument—or claim—has a certain persuasive power because of its rhetorical force, it begs the question: What, after all, is the basis for human dignity? And just why should such presumed dignity be honored?

John Stuart Mill (1806–78), the utilitarian, suggested an approach to the justification of human rights claims by grounding such claims in terms of general utility. Mill argued:

> To have a right, then, is, I conceive, to have some thing which society ought to defend me in the possession of. If the objector goes on to ask why it ought, I can give him no other reason than general utility.[94]

Rights, for Mill, are not a matter of abstract principles or of God's rules or natural law; rather, they are ways of thinking about freedom and actions which tend to bring about the greatest good for the greatest number. However, a person's right may be qualified. I may have the right to possess a certain property; but if the general happiness of the community would be enhanced by building a highway through my property, then my right to hold the property is trumped by the needs of the community. Whether this approach to human rights is successful will depend on whether or not utilitarianism can be defended.

Richard Rorty, a contemporary philosopher, questions whether we need to justify claims to human rights or any other moral claims.[95] Rorty supports human rights efforts as a way of developing a humane, secure, and prosperous human community. But he believes that this end is best achieved through what he calls a sentimental education rather than through argument and reasoning. The debates over just how to justify human rights in some theoretical way, he believes, have been endless and generally fruitless. Such debate, though reflecting careful analysis and reasoning, will do very little to change the heart or mind of those who violate human rights. What is needed, instead, is some way that helps us arrive at an emotional and personal identification with others. Respect for human beings and rights is best obtained, Rorty believes, through the main cultural instruments of literature, film, television and journalism. If Rorty is correct, then such programs as *Mr. Roger's Neighborhood* and *Sesame Street* are appropriate methods to achieve human rights and confer dignity. The creators of these programs certainly had that aim in mind. Many thinkers, however, believe that Rorty has abandoned the philosophical ship and is cast adrift in some kind of unfounded confidence that human emotions can lead to a better community.

In his *Social Philosophy*, Joel Feinberg searches for a justification of claims for human rights, but concludes that such rights claims are expressions of "attitudes." In contrast to Jefferson's language in the Declaration of Independence, Feinberg avoids grounding claims about human rights in religious assertions. Instead, he suggests that the idea of human worth expresses not so much some fact about human beings but rather an "attitude of respect—toward the humanity in each man's person." He then concludes:

> That attitude follows naturally from regarding everyone from the "human point of view," but is not grounded on anything more ultimate than itself, and is not demonstrably justifiable.[96]

The human rights skeptic might well ask Feinberg just what is the basis for holding this attitude of respect toward others. In this world it seems that far too few persons merit respect in terms of their actions and attitudes. In reference to the discussion of deep cultural intuitions in Chapter 7, it may be that Feinberg is drawing on just those intuitions.

In the two centuries between Jefferson and Feinberg, it appears that human rights have lost their status as truths rooted in the creative act of God and have become attitudes without any "demonstrable justification." Nevertheless, we can be assured that the dialogue will continue. The broad cultural support of the Black Lives Matter movement in 2020 reflected the significance of the concept of human rights. The very idea of human rights is both too deep and too precious to be relegated solely to the realms of attitude and emotions.

7

Why Be Moral?

If moral persons were not to eventually gain happiness, then morality, in the many cases where it brings no recompense on earth, would be just stupidity.

—C. J. Ducasse[97]

One of the things we ought to have learned from the history of moral philosophy is that the introduction of the word "intuition" by a moral philosopher is always a sign that something has gone badly wrong with the argument.

—Alasdair MacIntyre[98]

Why should I be moral? That question has a variety of possible interpretations. The question would be pointless if it asks for *moral* reasons for being moral. The real question is whether or not there are good reasons for being moral when such actions would entail some genuine cost to the individual choosing to act morally. In short, is there an inescapable conflict, at times, between rational self-interest and the demands of morality? This issue can be addressed by way of two related questions: 1) Why should *societies* develop some system of morality? 2) Why should any *individual* act morally?[99]

An answer to question 1) above, was given in Chapter 2 where I asserted that some type of system must of necessity be worked out in any society because of the conflicting wants, needs, and desires (WNDs) of people in that society. Societies must form some kind of moral patterns. I stipulated that any such system could properly be called a system of morality since the very point of morality is that of arbitrating such conflicts. Every society addresses those conflicts formally or informally, usually drawing on long religious traditions for justification. Such systems may, of course, be profoundly mistaken, yet the point of any such system is that of arbitrating conflicts of interests. In the animal kingdom such conflicts of interests are usually settled on the basis of power or other skills while human societies have used a variety of strategies—including the use of power. While I argued that any system which seeks to appropriately arbitrate among the conflicting WNDs should be designated as a system of morality, I left open the question of whether or not any of these systems can be rationally justified.

Proposing Rational Egoism

Why should any *individual* act morally? In addressing this question, the following lines of argument will be pursued. First, I shall claim, in contrast to a number of philosophers, that rational egoism is the primary moral principle. *Rational Egoism* maintains that the primary moral principle is the pursuit of the long-range goal of personal fulfillment (my formulation). The specific details of rational egoism in practice will depend on the belief system (worldview) held by the individual. Thus rational egoism in a religious context (e.g., Saint Augustine) would provide moral guidelines that would vary from rational egoism in a non-religious context (e.g., Epicurus). For Augustine, long-range personal fulfillment would involve the quest for Heaven and the beatific vision of God. For Epicurus, since death ends individual experience, personal fulfillment involves only the quest for pleasure during mortal life.

Next, I shall argue that "the moral point of view," as defended by several philosophers, is a dubious concept since it relies on intuitions rooted in a long cultural heritage. This cultural heritage that has shaped our intuitions may have provided what could be called a "received tradition" in morality; but this tradition cannot be identified as *the* moral point of view. Other traditions also exist that have shaped other sets of intuitions. Finally, an analysis of the role of sanctions—punishments and rewards—in moral systems will be pursued.

The distinction between rational egoism and moral duty can be expressed in the following way: rational egoism holds that pursuing one's own long-range self-interest is a completely rational motive for *any* action, while moral duty claims that there are times when our moral duty can, at least for some actions, override one's self-interest. This distinction exhibits the tension or contradiction between the two and represents the principal issue in many systems of morality that have been proposed.

Ronald Green, for instance, reflects this problem in his *Religious Reason* where he argues that it is rational for any society to construct principles and methods for settling conflicts and achieving cooperation (moral rules).[100] Nevertheless, he suggests that it is not necessarily rational for an individual member of such a society to sacrifice his or her own fulfillment in order to benefit the society as a whole. Green could cite the situation of a slave in a society where slavery was generally considered to be morally acceptable. Green maintains that this tension between what is rational for a society and what is rational for an individual has long been an issue in moral reasoning. His solution to this problem will be examined later in this chapter.

Self-interest vs. Duty

The apparent tension between rational self-interest and the call of moral duty is what underlines the significance of the question "Why should I be moral?" This question asks for a justification for being moral and implies that there may also be reasons for *not* being moral. The prudential justification of morality would claim that being moral is an important aspect of the quest for a fulfilling life; in short, it pays to be moral. A variety of non-prudential answers have been suggested such as "Because it is right," or "Because it is one's duty," or "Because one is obligated to be moral." These responses tend to beg the question and fail to give a complete answer since one can respond, "Why should I do what is right?" or "Why should I do my duty—if I have one?" or "Why should I do what I am obligated to do—if I am so obligated?" An answer putting an end to this sequence of "Whys" appears to be required.

The question "Why should I be moral?" could, for instance, be answered from a traditional religious position by claiming that God wills that I should be moral. However, one could ask "Just why should I do what God wills?" The response in this context surely would be "You should do what God wills because such obedience promises to be the path to the highest possible fulfillment and failing to do what God commands will lead to dire consequences." If one believes this response to be true, then the series of questions "But why should I—?" appears to come to a halt since it would seem odd to ask "But why should I pursue my highest possible fulfillment or seek to avoid dire consequences?" In general, the pursuit of happiness or the "good life" (in the non-moral sense of "good") seems not to need a rational justification. A variety of philosophers—Plato, Aristotle, Augustine, Aquinas—all held that persons naturally and appropriately seek happiness. This quest for happiness does not require some form of justification. There are differing views about what constitutes happiness or fulfillment; nevertheless, such pursuit seems rational by its very nature.

Some might object that this prudential justification of religious morality is not in keeping with traditions that urge self-sacrifice and self-forgetting. A response by W. D. Hudson calls such an objection into question:

> Is it not significant that those who advocate self-sacrifice usually present it as a path to self-realization? "He that loses his life shall find it"? However difficult it may be to make sense of this, and I do not personally find it difficult, the fact remains that to those who advocate it, and to those who heed them, self-sacrifice appears to be a duty because it is the way to some kind of self-realization.[101]

Each philosopher reviewed in Chapter 4 who supported a moral code or principle argued that the path to human fulfillment is also the moral pathway—as the individual thinker envisioned fulfillment and the moral pathway. In none of them was there, finally, a tension between doing what is moral and doing what is in the long-term best interest of the self. All of them, of course, would have granted that there may be times when an action that might serve immediate self-interest should be avoided since that action would undercut long-term self-interest. Thieving my neighbor's Twinkie or Porsche may meet my immediate self-interests, but the long-range results may be costly to me. Reason can serve the aims of long-range self-interest by helping us to see the consequences of certain actions. In Hume's terms, reason can help show us the way to get what we truly desire.

Rational Egoism Is Not Selfishness

Rational egoism, however, is not to be identified with selfishness. To clarify this point, distinctions need to be made among self-interested, selfish, self-referential, and altruistic acts. A *selfish* act is one pursued *only* for the interests of the self without any regard for the interests of others. A *self-interested* act is one pursued for one's own interest but may or may not include concern for the interest of others. A *self-referential* act is one pursued for the interests of another while it also has a self-interested component. For example, a parent spending a sleepless night nursing a sick child through a crisis is positively interested in the child's welfare, but is also clearly pursuing a *self-interested* activity though not a *selfish* one. The child's flourishing is a significant aspect of the parent's own flourishing. A deed which contributes to the welfare of another in this way is certainly not a selfish deed, but it can be self-referential if it also contributes to the interests of the one performing the deed.

Altruistic Actions

Such self-referential acts should be distinguished from *purely altruistic* ones in that a purely altruistic act demonstrates concern for the welfare of others without any regard for one's own welfare or interests. Hence a purely altruistic act would have no self-referential dimensions whatsoever. The phrase "purely altruistic" is used here since "altruism" is often defined as "unselfish concern for the welfare of others." But such a definition does not clearly distinguish between a concern for others that has a self-referential component and one without such a component.

With these definitions in place, my thesis of rational egoism would maintain that unselfish but self-referential actions can be rationally grounded, but purely altruistic deeds cannot be rationally grounded *if* such a deed also undercuts the long-range fulfillment of the actor. A purely altruistic deed that has no impact on the long-range fulfillment of the actor could not, on the other hand, be considered to be "immoral." In short, it is never rational to act in such a way as to increase the welfare of another at a net cost to one's own long range self-interest—which would include one's interests in the welfare of those about whom I care. Recall that parental investment in a child's welfare, for instance, is also in the self-interests of the parent.

Morality Is *For* Us

Central to this work is the claim that "morality is for us" in that the moral pathway always promises fulfillment and is, therefore, fully compatible with rational egoism. To defend this assertion, I first make a bald appeal to the authority of a number of philosophers. Chapter 4 demonstrated that the major theories of morality, religious or non-religious, always claim that the moral pathway is, in fact, the fulfilling pathway. The nature of the "fulfillment" envisioned differed considerably, however, among these theories. Plato, for instance, argued that the wise person is the good person since the wise person is just and the just soul is the most fulfilled soul. Aristotle argued that every action is thought to aim at some good and that what people aim at intrinsically is the good of a human being as human being. His theory of ethics is an elaboration on the quest for personal fulfillment by way of human "excellence." Epicurus advised that the proper goal of the individual is that of pleasure for the self within the limits of our mortal life span. Augustine and Aquinas, who shaped much of Christian theology, held that the moral pathway is always part of the journey toward eternal bliss in God's presence. Jeremy Bentham and J. S. Mill, the founders of Utilitarianism, were both psychological egoists in claiming, as Bentham put it, that "Nature has placed mankind under the governance of two sovereign masters, pain and pleasure. It is for them alone to point out what we ought to do, as well as *determine* what we *shall* do" (my emphasis).[102] Bentham informs us that physical, political, moral, and religious sanctions teach us to be good Utilitarians as we *necessarily* seek to maximize our own pleasure. Finally, Immanuel Kant, though arguing that the truly moral deed is one done solely because it was morally binding, maintained that the very idea of morality includes the conviction that the morally good person will be rewarded and the evil person punished. To sustain this claim, Kant needed to *posit* freedom of the will, the immortality of the soul, and the existence of God.

While this persistent link between the moral pathway and personal fulfillment does not appear to be some form of logical entailment, it does appear to be a highly rational reading of the human venture. What rational person, for instance, would find any interest in a suggested moral pathway if that pathway promised only that you would suffer and be discarded for no good purpose? No moral philosopher ever held to such a theory—probably well aware that no person would find this position either attractive or rationally compelling. Richard Taylor made this point nicely:

> However one approaches ethics—whether from the ancient standpoint of virtue, or the modern one of duty, or from any other—what one finally asserts has to be something that makes a difference and this, in the last analysis, must be a difference with respect to human happiness. Otherwise, whatever is said will be simply pointless.[103]

Challenges to Rational Egoism

There are, of course, philosophers who would challenge my contention that rational egoism is the primary moral principle. Some argue that rational egoism is contradictory to the very concept of morality and thus cannot be a *moral* principle. William Frankena, for instance, in his criticism of ethical egoism, maintains that "living wholly by the principle of enlightened self-love (my "rational egoism") just is not a kind of *morality*."[104] Frankena also claims that the moral point of view is *disinterested*, not *interested*. Frankena appears to maintain that, while self-interest is not necessarily immoral, true morality moves beyond any kind of self-interest, even of self-referential actions that are not selfish. Evidently the parent caring for the sick child is not demonstrating morality since the parent's actions are clearly interested, not disinterested. Frankena would not claim that the parent was being immoral even if the act would evidently not classify as a truly moral one. Instead, he would hold that such actions are to be seen as morally neutral.

Other philosophers commonly understand the term "moral" in a way that would reject rational egoism as a possible *moral* theory. John Mackie implies this when he writes, "Morality has the function of checking what would be the natural result of prudence alone."[105] Mackie's "prudence" would carry much the same meaning as my "rational egoism." David Gauthier makes much the same point:

> Morality is a system of principles such that it is advantageous for everyone if everyone accepts and acts on it, yet acting on the system of principles requires that some perform disadvantageous acts.[106]

In those passages, neither Mackie nor Gauthier commit themselves to the proposition that morality may require actions that are *long-term* disadvantageous. Short-term disadvantage would be acceptable to practically all moral theories if such disadvantage is needed for long-term advantage of fulfillment. I might, for instance, spend time and effort to help someone get their car out of the snow. The immediate disadvantage is clear though in the long-term I could consider such actions to be part of what I should do to be seen as a virtuous person in my community. I could also hope that my actions may influence others who could, some day, be of help to me. Furthermore, such actions would support my own self-image as a virtuous person and, therefore, help confirm an image of myself as a good human being—an image that might well support my sense of fulfillment.

A more direct illustration would be that of various saints from a variety of religious traditions who obviously forego, through vows of poverty and celibacy, what many of us would consider to be advantageous experiences. Yet those taking such vows always understand them to be part of the pathway that leads to ultimate fulfillment. For such saints, long-term advantage requires what some would judge to be short-term "sacrifice."

Another philosopher, Kurt Baier, argues,

> being moral is following rules designed to overrule self-interest whenever it is in the interest of everyone alike that everyone should set aside his interest.[107]

Baier appears to argue that morality contributes to advantage in a way that prudence, alone, cannot. Yet his claim that "it is in the interest of everyone alike" to overrule self-interest has an air of paradox about it for the claim would apply also to the one who is *overruling* his or her self-interests for *the sake of his or her self-interest*. It is, apparently, in my self-interest to overrule self-interest. But the issue, again, is whether or not Baier is thinking of short-term or long-term interests. Most would agree that it would be rational to sacrifice some dimensions of self-interest on some occasions if that "sacrifice" would promote one's long-term advantage. If that is Baier's contention, then his position is not in conflict with the rational egoism I am promoting. In his *Practical Ethics*, Peter Singer rejects ethical egoism for similar reasons. "A justification (of ethical standards) in terms of self-interest alone will not do. . . . for the notion of ethics carries with it the idea of something bigger than the individual."[108]

It could be argued, from a rather cynical perspective, that those who hold that morality can involve self-sacrifice are those who seek to avoid such self-sacrifice themselves while urging "moral duty" upon others—e.g., those who find ways of avoiding the military while hoping that others will take on the moral duty of possible self-sacrifice. Could it be that those who die in battle to protect a nation are suckers or losers? I hasten to add that I am not accusing the philosophers mentioned of such cynicism. It does seem clear, however, that nations and cultures do find ways of encouraging men and women to risk their lives "for their country." This encouragement includes not only the threat of sanctions on those who refuse the call, but also to formulating ideas of bravery, honor, and heroism that help make the risk of self-sacrifice worthwhile and a comfort for gold-star parents.

Moral Intuitionism

Frankena, Mackie, Gauthier, Baier, and Singer all reflect what could be called a "received tradition" in moral thought and in this way represent a type of moral intuitionism. In ethical theory, intuitionism holds that the good or the right thing to do can be known directly through some faculty of intuition. None of the five present *arguments* designed to show that morality must be disinterested or must involve an overruling of self-interest, nor do they stipulate some definition of "morality" that would involve such consideration. Instead, they *claim* that this is what "moral" or "morality" means or implies; and in doing so they reflect a type of intuitionism that just "sees" morality in that way. Fully developed forms of ethical intuitionism are generally rejected at this point in history. It is rejected, in part, because there seems to be no way of adjudicating between conflicting sets of intuitions—as when the intuitions of X conflict with the intuitions of Y. Furthermore, it is difficult to identify just what this faculty of intuition might be. When a philosopher falls back on claims of intuition to support a position, I suggest that their arguments have gone wrong—as MacIntyre claims in the epigraph to this chapter.

It may be that most persons in our modern Western culture do share what appear to be certain moral intuitions. These intuitions are usually similar to the content of our conscience. Nevertheless, surely such intuitions have been shaped by certain cultural traditions that have made their way into our moral language and consciousness. They are not insights into the fundamental and objective nature of morality. Furthermore, these intuitions run strongly counter to a variety of moral theories that have been presented throughout history. Epicurus, for instance, clearly argued that self-interest is the central principle of morality as he saw it. I would add that his moral philosophy is found in all works that deal seriously with the history of ethics, thereby indicating that the authors of such works consider Epicurus's egoistic hedonism to be a *moral theory*—in spite of Frankena's claim that it is "just not a kind of morality." Aristotle's ethical theory would also reject the claim that true morality may result in some long-term cost to some of those who walk the moral pathway. Finally, Bentham and J. S. Mill, the founders of Utilitarianism, both held to psychological egoism—the theory that we of necessity always choose those actions that we believe to be in our self-interest. They argued that various sanctions would eventually shape us into being good utilitarians as we discover how our true self-interests could best be met. The point, then, is that the history of moral philosophy suggests that "moral" is not limited to the meanings that Frankena, Mackie, Gauthier, and Baier suggest. They draw on a received tradition that has shaped their intuitions. This tradition will be explored later in this chapter.

The "Moral Point of View"

A similar challenge to my position that reflects another form of intuitionism is found in the concept of "the moral point of view." One such position is explored by William Frankena in his *Ethics*, where he develops an analysis of "the moral point of view."[109] In another essay, Frankena puts the point bluntly: "I believe . . . that morality requires genuine sacrifice, and may even require self-sacrifice."[110] Later Frankena makes a significant observation:

> It seems clear to me . . . that a universal coincidence of being moral and achieving the best score can be shown to be false—unless it is posited that there is a hereafter in which God will readjust the balance.[111]

Given his understanding of what constitutes true morality, Frankena's observation is fully compatible with the theory presented in this book. Kant anticipated Frankena's point and proceeded to posit that the existence of God is necessary if morality, as he understood it, is to be rational.

Another characterization of "the moral point of view" was proposed by Kurt Baier. He held:

> . . . one is taking *the moral point of view* (my emphasis) if one is not being egoistic, one is doing things on principle, and one is willing to universalize one's principles, and in doing so considers the good of everyone alike.[112]

A similar position is taken by Peter Singer in his analysis of "the ethical point of view" by linking this view to universalizing:

> But what is "the ethical point of view"? I have suggested that a distinguishing feature of ethics is that ethical judgments are universalisable. Ethics requires us to go beyond our own personal point of view to a standpoint like that of the impartial spectator who takes a universal point of view.[113]

I note that Frankena, Baier, and Singer write of *the* moral point of view—not *a* moral point of view—thereby implying that it is possible to formulate something like a universally true, objective, and rationally grounded "moral point of view." Perhaps there is some Platonic Form of "moral" that these philosophers have contemplated.

Only Frankena's position will be analyzed at this point since his position reflects the central claims of those who defend something like "the moral point of view." Several features of his "moral point of view" are parallel to aspects of my own position. I agree with Frankena on the following: 1) Reasons for moral judgments involve facts about just how an action would affect the lives of sentient beings in terms of the distribution of non-moral good and evil. In other words, moral judgments involve appropriate arbitration among various competing wants, needs, and desires—WNDs. 2) When the judgment is about oneself or one's own actions, the facts about just how one's actions or disposition affects the lives of other sentient beings are part of the consideration.

Universalizing Principle

A central factor, however, in Frankena's description of "*the* moral point of view" is problematic, namely his claim that in making a moral judgment one must be willing to universalize that judgment. In this, Frankena follows the language of Kant, Baier and others. Let us call this the "universalizing principle." The difficulty with this principle involves at least two concerns. First, the "precise nature and definition (of this principle), and the implications it has for moral reasoning, are disputed."[114] Second, the justification of the principle is not clear. The claim seems to be presented as a self-evident truth. An extended discussion of these concerns is beyond the intentions and range of this work. I will, instead, outline the major reasons why I call into question the validity of claiming that the "universalizing principle" and the "moral point of view" are necessary conditions for a moral judgment.

The Roots of Universalizing

The central meaning of the universalizing principle is that one cannot make oneself an exception to some moral rule or judgment. According to this principle, if I make the moral judgment that some act X is morally wrong for Mr. Z to do, then I must also judge that I would also be morally culpable if I carried out X. The idea of universalizability is clearly related to the ideas of fairness and impartiality. I must judge my own actions by the same standards that I use to judge the actions of others. Furthermore, I cannot claim special considerations just because of certain factors in my own biography such as race, family lineage, national identity, religious beliefs or lack thereof, educational status, etc. Another human being has equal moral status with me purely on the grounds that they are human beings.

With notable exceptions—such as racism—this intuition of fairness and impartiality is so deeply imprinted in our cultural heritage that to question it seems odd if not outright absurd. I maintain, however, that the universalizing principle that underlies this sense of fairness is, itself, based on intuitions rooted in thought forms and moral theories that have shaped our culture. Universalizing, therefore, is not some objective principle somehow rooted in the structures of human rationality or language. In other words, the universalizing principle reflects a worldview or metaphysical vision that provides the context within which such universalizing can be seen as rational.

In Chapter 1, the claim was made that the substance of a morality rooted in theistic religious traditions cannot be successfully defended on non-theistic or naturalistic foundations. One approach to a defense of that claim was made in Chapter 6 where the ability of theistic traditions to move beyond narrow tribalism to a universal affirmation of all human beings was analyzed. That analysis resulted in a mixed review. The concept of God as creator of all human beings would appear to imply that all human beings essentially belong to the same tribe. The Quakers have held to that conviction. However, the analysis given in that chapter also noted that theistic traditions can also be tragically divisive.

On the other hand, purely naturalistic systems, such as those of Aristotle, Epicurus, and Nietzsche, provide little or no basis for such universalizing. The mere *fact* that all human beings are equally the product of natural forces, such as evolution, does not logically entail the *moral* proposition that all persons should be equally respected or fairly treated.

The Concept of Justice

I have claimed that the universalizing principle reflects a worldview or metaphysical vision that provides the context within which such universalizing can be seen as rational. A further defense of this claim can be linked to the concept of justice as it developed in Western thought. Alasdair MacIntyre has noted the contrast in the scope of justice from the ancient Greek (fifth or fourth century, BCE) view to that reflected in modern liberal thought.

> For a modern liberal the norms of justice are to govern the relationships of human beings as such; . . . For Aristotle, by contrast, justice properly so-called is exercised between free and equal citizens of one and the same *polis* (political community, as a city-state).[115]

The scope of justice for modern liberalism is universal in that differences in political societies, social status, racial identity, or other boundaries are viewed as irrelevant in any given transaction. Persons must be respected as persons. For Aristotle and other Greeks, justice is confined to the boundaries of a particular *polis*, and the content of justice varied with social and citizenship boundaries. Doing justice may mean treating others as is their *due*, but the sticky issue is always that of deciding the content of what *is* due. What was due to those whom Aristotle viewed as natural slaves differed substantially from what was due to the land-owning and aristocratic citizen of Athens. Some Greeks, it seems, found various levels of tribalism to be a natural part of their theory of justice.

Justice Beyond the *Polis*

When justice extended beyond the *polis* in the ancient world, it appears to have required a theology. Socrates, for instance, appealed to the unwritten laws made by God when acknowledging that the scope of justice could move beyond the boundaries of the *polis*. The Stoics developed a notable extension in theory and practice. They were the first thinkers in the Greco-Roman world to assert that the scope of justice is all of humanity. They made this claim because they believed that every human being is a member of one and the same community under one and the same law.

Stoics on "Justice"

The Stoic claim that all human beings are under the umbrella of *humanity* is based on their notion that God is in everything as a force and rationality that pervades all. The Stoic conception of God was not that of some entity in a single location but as a rational substance that exists in all things and controls not only the structure of nature but also the events in the world.

This view of God pervading and directing the universe led to the Stoic attitude of acceptance of things as they are. Epictetus reflected this attitude in saying, "Demand not that events should happen as you wish, but wish them to happen as they do happen."[116] The Stoics held that the soul of the human being is also part of God as a divine spark, and human reason is rooted in the divine *logos* or reason. This universal participation in the divine provides the basis for the universal application of justice—which is divine—to all persons. Cicero makes a Stoic point in claiming, "this whole world is one city to be conceived of as including gods and human beings."[117] Since divine reason pervades and directs events, then this reason is reflected in the ruling status of Rome and the laws of the community. The duties reflected in these laws and customs varied with relationships. As Cicero explained:

> Our highest duties are to parents and fatherland (patria), that state in which we have citizenship; next come children and the rest of the immediate family; then remoter kin; and finally those friends who deserve well of us.[118]

Here, again, the old patterns of tribalism appear.

One limitation to this Stoic view of justice and law is found in their identification of the standard Roman law and practice with this universal divine justice. According to the Stoics, such laws apply to all persons but there existed no means of criticizing those laws. There was no reference point outside that law by which to bring criticism of that law. It appears that any conception of justice that extends beyond the polis to all humankind must have some source to make that possible. There must also be some source by which to judge the laws of a particular polis.

This source, MacIntyre claims, is the Abrahamic history and the development of the Torah as divine commands. What the Torah in its developed form brings is not only specific details (as in the Ten Commandments) but also a sense of justice that is not restricted to Israel. Justice is expressed as a law holding for all nations. MacIntyre traces the development of this law conception of morality through Saint Paul and the Christian tradition with special focus on Saint Augustine's analysis of the universal law of love. In quoting Saint Paul, Augustine presents love as the divine *standard* for justice "so as to owe no one anything but to love one another"(Rom 3:18). In his commentary on 1 John 4:4–12, Augustine provides what is perhaps the shortest moral rule ever given: "Love, and do what you will."[119]

This review is not designed to show that the line traced into Christian history is the *correct* understanding of justice. That question is left open. What is suggested, however, is that the modern liberal view of justice with its call for the universalizing principle and its emphasis on fairness and impartiality has its roots in this history. For good or ill, this long history of Christian thought has made its way deeply into Western culture and has shaped our intuitions about morality and justice so deeply that these intuitions strike us as either common sense or patently obvious. When Kant, for instance, writes of the "very idea of morality," he clearly reflects the Protestant tradition in which he was nurtured even though he seeks to ground this morality in human reason as such. Kant seems to confuse his intuitions with what he claims to be the objective structures of reason. His own dependency on this religious tradition becomes transparent when he argues that freedom of the will, eternal life, and God must be *posited* if morality is to be rational. Given his view of morality, small wonder that those posits were developed. If one begins with a view of morality shaped by a theistic tradition, it would not be surprising to justify it by appealing to a form of theism. Philosopher Ronald Green makes a claim parallel to Kant's by arguing that our given understanding of the nature of morality will finally require reason to posit a religious worldview.[120]

Universalization Without Religion

In contrast, if one begins with Aristotle's ethics or the moral views of Epicurus, "moral reason" would hardly lead to religious belief. More contemporary philosophers, when speaking of "the moral point of view," are also drawing on this religiously rooted tradition for content even though they may be rejecting the theology which originally developed and sustained it. Their construction of "the moral point of view," I claim, ends up being a form of intuitionism rooted in a long cultural heritage. These philosophers keep the universalizing principle but seek to justify it on some basis other than religious belief. The question remains, however, whether or not the attempt can be successful.

Other philosophers have argued in similar fashion that the content of most of our moral terms has been shaped by Western religious traditions and that these terms have become meaningless or even harmful when the religious beliefs are given up. G. E. M. Anscombe argued both that Christianity constructed the law conception of ethics from the Torah and that the long dominance of Christian ethics has deeply embedded this conception in our language and thought.

> (T)he concepts of obligation, and duty . . . and of what is *morally* right and wrong, and of the *moral* sense of "ought," ought to be jettisoned, if this is psychologically possible, because they are survivals, or derivatives from survivals, from an earlier conception of ethics which no long generally survives, and are only harmful without it.[121]

Richard Taylor puts his case directly:

> Religion introduced the idea of right and wrong at a higher level than that resulting from human custom and law, namely, one resulting from divine law. Modern philosophy thenceforth *kept* the distinction between moral right and wrong, making it the pivotal idea of moral philosophy, but cast aside the context that gave it meaning, namely God's will.[122]

Since Taylor rejects the idea of God, he argues for a return to the Greek view of ethics as the pursuit of a life of "excellence," rather than an ethic of duty. He brings Aristotle's view back into the modern world.

The Role of Sanctions

The question "Why be moral?" leads to a consideration of the role of sanctions, rewards, or punishments in morality. Given my theory about moral theories as developed throughout this work, sanctions represent an inescapable aspect of morality. I have claimed, for instance, that all major moral theories have maintained that the moral pathway is the most fulfilling pathway. That claim would evidently entail the view that failure to walk the moral pathway would in some way undercut or hinder life fulfillment. Such an entailment can be discerned in the moral theories reviewed in Chapter 4. Representative voices can be cited. Plato argued that the unjust soul could not be a contented soul. Failure to follow the ethical pathway, Aristotle maintained, would result in a life that falls below excellence. Even Epicurus, with his egoistic hedonism, would claim that failure to follow his moral advice would lead to more pain and less pleasure. And the major traditions of religious ethics are filled with promises of rewards and/or punishments: Heaven and Hell (traditional Judaism, Christianity, and Islam), reincarnation in lower forms of life (Hinduism), failure to find peace (Buddhism).

A variety of thinkers have linked serious morality to the idea of God as the final arbiter of justice in terms of reward and punishment. In his *Laws*, Plato held that belief in God was necessary for the maintenance of a stable and just community. A long line of theologians and religious philosophers, including Augustine, Aquinas, Maimonides, and John Calvin, maintained a similar position. Even Sigmund Freud—no supporter of religious views—believed that the threat of religious-based sanctions did, in fact, help restrain some of the nastier elements of human nature. John Locke, the seventeenth-century English philosopher, although not an orthodox religious thinker, believed that one had little basis for trusting an atheist. Jeremy Bentham and J. S. Mill, who shaped utilitarianism, both held—at least in writing—that sanctions delivered by God helped to make good utilitarians out of self-interested human beings. Even Thomas Jefferson, the enlightenment deist of the eighteenth century, held that "no system of morality however pure it might be" could survive "without the sanction of divine authority stampt upon it."[123]

This history of reflection on morality suggests that any system of morality would lose not only its point but its seriousness if sanctions were not part of the moral pathway prescribed. Morality may be "for us," but moral failure would appear to be "against us."

To be sure, many moderns no longer take divine sanctions seriously; however, most still take into account that sanctions may still be delivered by other human beings if they detect what they deem as your evil acts and if they have the power to level sanctions against you.[124] Nevertheless, if one has sufficient power or stealth, the threat of human sanctions can be largely diminished. The theory of divine sanctions, on the other hand, contains a dimension not to be found in sanctions delivered only by other human beings. We may be able to deceive others or we may have sufficient power to save us from sanctions delivered by other human beings. Divine sanctions, however, would be quite a different story. One cannot escape from the eyes of God nor hope to deceive God. Given God's power, God also has the final say about the matter. In his *God Is Watching You*, Dominic Johnson traces evidence from a number of sciences and concludes that our evolutionary heritage has left within us a deep sense of being seen by God and that we will eventually have our case reviewed by Heavenly powers.[125] There appears to be strong evidence showing that this sense of divine sanctions does, in fact, have strong influence over human behavior.

In closing, my claim that the "universalizing principle" is rooted in religious traditions does not imply that the principle and its religious roots are rationally justified. That remains an open question in this book.

8

Ethical Relativism

> If your heart does not want a world of moral reality, your head will assuredly never make you believe in one.
> —William James[126]

THE GREAT DIVERSITY OF moral codes has puzzled philosophers and others over the centuries. Protagoras (ca. 490–421 BCE) sought to solve this puzzle by asserting that there is no moral code existing which properly applies to all human beings at all times and in all places. He held that peoples have their own moral codes, but they cannot claim to have a code that is universally applicable. This was an early formulation of ethical relativism, a theory which still attracts followers and generates lively discussions in most introductory courses in ethics.

Ethical Relativism: A Philosophical Issue

Ethical relativism is an example of a typical philosophical issue in three ways. First, it is clearly not a scientific problem since it cannot be solved on the basis of purely empirical evidence. Second, it is an issue where some progress in the debate can often be made by way of analysis and argument. Compelling argument can be constructed even though such arguments are not rooted in the hard facts of scientific observation. Finally, the issue is philosophical in that much of the time the debate involves both a careful clarification of terms and an analysis of the logical implications of certain beliefs. To call it philosophical, of course, neither glorifies nor demeans the issue; it merely identifies the nature of the theory and the processes needed to arrive at a rational solution—if there is one.

Defining Ethical Relativism

Since debate on this issue often results from confusion about terms, some clarifications will be helpful. One way of clarifying ethical relativism is to contrast it with its opposite theory—ethical absolutism. Ethical absolutism holds that there is at least one moral rule or principle that properly and objectively applies to any person at any place and at any time. Ethical absolutism does not claim that persons know these rules or principles nor do persons necessarily follow such rules and principles. Many ethical absolutists make claim to such knowledge, but it is possible to hold to ethical absolutism without claiming to know what the right moral rules might be.

The ethical relativist, on the other hand, asserts that there are no moral rules or principles which properly and objectively apply to any person at any time and at any place. The relativist grants that there are moral rules of various kinds, because every culture reflects some kind of moral guidelines. However, the moral rules held in one culture do not represent rules that would morally obligate a differing culture. Every culture has its own moral guidelines. Most relativists also grant that some moral rules can properly be seen as the *right* or *correct* moral rules in that the moral rules generally adopted by a culture are, in fact, the *right* moral rules for that culture. However, the right moral rules for culture A are not necessarily the right rules for culture B. Furthermore, for the ethical relativist, these are the only moral rules that exist since there are no objective universal moral rules that can be used to evaluate the moral rules held by various cultures.

Cultural Relativism

Another theory—cultural relativism—needs to be identified in order to avoid confusion. Sometimes called "descriptive relativism," cultural relativism is the theory that moral values and rules do, in fact, vary from culture to culture. Some cultures, for example, allow for the holding of slaves while other cultures do not. Cultural relativism is not a philosophical issue; instead, it is a purely descriptive claim that can be tested by examining various cultures to see if differences in moral codes do exist. Social scientists generally agree that the theory of cultural relativism is true. However, even if cultural relativism is true, that fact does not entail the conclusion that ethical relativism is also true. This point will be clarified in the following pages.

Absolutisms: Rule and Principle

A distinction between *principle* absolutism and *rule* absolutism is important. A *rule* absolutist holds that there are some specific rules that always morally obligate all persons. Lying, for instance, can be seen as always morally wrong. On the other hand, a *principle* absolutist holds that there is a basic moral principle that always obligates, but that some specific moral rules may not always obligate. "Always do the loving act" is one candidate for principle absolutism. This principle can override or trump a specific moral rule at times. For instance, there may be times when telling a lie is the loving thing to do in some specific situation. For instance, one could be morally justified in lying to the Nazis if they ask if you are harboring Jews on your premises.

The Utilitarian principle, "Always pursue those actions which produce the greatest good for the greatest number," is also a principle absolute. Even the advice of Epicurus, "Always do what maximizes your own pleasure and minimizes your own pain," is also a principle absolute. It is clear that principle absolutists do not always agree about the nature of the principle to be followed. Non-religious thinkers as well as religious thinkers can be principle absolutists.

Ethical Relativism: Two Forms

There are also two forms of ethical relativism: 1) *cultural* ethical relativism and 2) *individual* ethical relativism. Both are ethical relativists since both claim that there are no absolute moral principles or rules that properly obligate all persons. The *cultural* ethical relativist holds that the right moral rules for any culture are the rules that are generally accepted by all in that culture. If persons in a culture generally agree that slavery is morally acceptable, then slavery is, in fact, morally acceptable in that culture.

The *individual* ethical relativist, on the other hand, asserts that the individual is the proper judge of moral actions. The right moral rules for any individual are the rules *believed* to be right by that person. The rules generally believed to be right by others in that culture do nor obligate the individual in that culture. Furthermore, the moral rules believed to be right by one person are not necessarily right for others in that culture.

Arguments Supporting Ethical Relativism

An argument often used in support of *cultural* ethical relativism is the argument from *cultural* relativism. Some form of this argument was proposed by Protagoras. This argument maintains that since varying cultures hold varying moral beliefs (cultural relativism), it follows that ethical relativism must be true. Upon inspection, this argument fails. While cultural relativism, as a descriptive theory, is probably true, it could still be the case that an absolute moral principle or rule does exist. By analogy, even though varying cultures have held varying theories about the shape of the solar system, that variation would not imply that there is no correct (absolute) theory regarding the solar system. The heliocentric view has largely come to prevail as the correct theory.

It follows that one culture may, in fact, hold to a truly absolute moral system. Or perhaps there is an absolute moral system which exists but which has not yet been fully comprehended or followed by any person or culture. A variety of religious moral systems would claim to hold to a moral system that is absolute in its extent, even though these religious thinkers admit that other cultures hold differing views. Other cultures are just mistaken, the absolutist could claim. At this point, cultural ethical relativism needs further arguments in its favor.

A second argument in support of ethical relativism could be called the *argument from lack of proof*. Since no one has successfully shown that ethical absolutism is true, then ethical relativism in some form must be true. Refutation of this argument is straightforward. The mere fact that a theory has not been conclusively proven to be true does not entail that the theory is false. For example, by the twelfth century no one had conclusively proven that the solar system is heliocentric, yet that lack of proof did not entail that the theory was false. Furthermore, a number of philosophers have maintained that they have sufficient evidence to support some form of ethical absolutism. A variety of thinkers reviewed in Chapter 4 made such a claim. While the argument from lack of proof may fail as an argument, its conclusion could still be true—just not *proven* to be true.

A third argument in support of ethical relativism has ancient roots. Offered by Protagoras, this argument could be called the *argument from practical benefit*. While Protagoras noted that varying cultures had varying moral rules, he argued that the moral views generally held by a culture are the right ones for that culture since these rules help the people of that culture to survive and flourish. The argument raises a number of questions.

First, it may be that the rules prevailing in a culture are not necessarily rules that help that culture to flourish. There may be other rules that would be even more helpful toward such flourishing. Some moral reforms might be helpful. That seems to be an open question. Finally, the argument assumes a premise that reflects ethical absolutism. To claim that the moral rules of a culture are right for that culture *because* they help that culture to flourish is to infer an absolutist claim: "Any culture at any time or place *ought* to follow those moral rules which help that culture to flourish." A relativist who makes such a claim does so at the cost of abandoning ethical relativism. Such a relativist sets forth a criterion by which the moral system of a culture can be analyzed, criticized and reformed.

Another argument offered in support of ethical relativism could be called the *argument from tolerance*. The argument grows out of the perception that systems of moral absolutism seem intolerant, narrow, and inflexible. Certain religious traditions could be accused of such intolerance. This argument raises a number of issues. In a certain sense, any system of morality reflects some kind of "intolerance" in the sense that such a system opposes moral practices that run against the system. Moral systems are always gatekeepers; their aim is to be intolerant toward some actions. Furthermore, there are a number of absolutist systems that reflect a good deal of tolerance. The Utilitarian theory reflects a good deal of tolerance, as do religious systems that emphasize compassion or love for the neighbor. Finally, the argument from tolerance reflects a closet absolutist view. It infers that tolerance is an *absolute* moral principle that ought to be generally honored.

A purely logical point should now be made. Even though the arguments in support of ethical relativism appear to have failed, the theory could still be true. A failed argument fails only to *prove* that the conclusion is true, but the conclusion of the argument could still be true. The conclusion of an argument may still be true even if the argument form is invalid and the premises are false. Some beliefs may be true even if we cannot supply arguments or evidence to prove they are true. Religious beliefs often rely on that logical point. Nevertheless, many persons prefer to have *knowledge* supported by evidence and sound argument, not just belief.

Arguments in Support of Ethical Absolutism

If arguments supporting ethical relativism are not compelling, are there any cogent arguments which demonstrate that ethical absolutism is true or that ethical relativism is false? One conclusive approach would be to *prove* that a particular form of ethical absolutism is true. As Chapter 4 illustrated, many thinkers from Plato to contemporaries have attempted to do just that; however, any such attempt would be beyond the intentions of this chapter or this book. Hence, arguments here will be limited to those that attempt to show that ethical relativism must be false. If this attempt is successful, then some form of ethical absolutism must be true—leaving open the question of just which form might be true. Three lines of argument will be pursued. The first will seek to show that ethical relativism is incoherent upon analysis. The second will offer a number of *reductio ad absurdum* arguments against ethical relativism. Finally, the suggestion that ethical relativists are really closet egoists will be explored.

Ethical Relativism Is Incoherent

Upon analysis, ethical relativism appears to be incoherent in making the claim—as some relativists do—that the *right* moral rules for a culture are the rules generally *believed* to be right by the people of that culture. But what coherent connection can be made between the fact that a culture believes some rules to be the right rules and the claim that such rules are, therefore, the right moral rules for that culture. How does the mere fact of "believing" that some X is right entail the claim that X is, in fact, right?

This question leads to an attempt to impale the ethical relativist on the "horns of a dilemma." It seems that the ethical relativist must hold either (first horn) that there are *good reasons* for the persons of that culture to hold the moral beliefs that they do, or (second horn) there are no such *good reasons*. If relativists assert the first horn and claim there are good reasons to support the moral beliefs of a culture, then they are committed to some form of absolutism. For if the relativists grant that *good reasons* can be given, these reasons would surely justify the same kind of moral rules for any culture. By analogy: If good reasons for holding belief B can be given, then others should be led to hold B to be true. If good reasons justify an action, then the same reasons would justify the same action for others. Furthermore, if such good reasons exist for some moral beliefs, then these reasons establish objective justifications for such moral beliefs. In short, some form of absolutism has been established.

Consider the second horn of the dilemma. Perhaps there are no good reasons for a culture to hold the moral views that they do. But if there are no *good reasons* for holding such beliefs, on what grounds can the relativist claim that such beliefs are *right* for that culture? It appears that we are left with the claim that such rules are right even if there are no good reasons for believing that they are right. Yet it would seem absurd to claim that certain moral rules are the right moral rules merely because a culture happened—without good reasons—to believe what they believe. Such a position would seem to be a desperate view of the human quest for moral guidance.

The Moral Nihilist

There is the position of the moral nihilist who would claim there are no such things as coherent moral facts or moral rules. However, even the moral nihilist is forced to make life decisions regarding the two issues traced in this work: 1) What is the most fulfilling life that a rational person could pursue? 2) As persons seek their fulfillment, do they have any obligation to aid others in their quest for fulfillment? Nihilists must answer those questions in living out their lives whether or not they identify those questions as moral in nature. In short, they are condemned to be moral agents as they live and choose.

Reductio ad Absurdum Arguments

Various *reductio ad absurdum* arguments have been offered to refute ethical relativism. These arguments attempt to show that since ethical relativism leads to absurd implications, the theory itself must be absurd. These arguments tend to draw on intuitions that we hold.

Reductio: If individual ethical relativism is true, then it follows that individuals cannot be mistaken in their moral judgments. But it seems absurd to maintain that individuals can never be mistaken in their moral judgments; therefore, individual ethical relativism must be absurd. For example, if individual ethical relativism is true, then Adolph Hitler could not have been wrong in his moral judgments. Furthermore, if individual ethical relativism is true, then Adolph Hitler would be the moral equal of Saint Francis or the Buddha. These conclusions appear to be absurd.

Individual ethical relativism also generates a curious implication. Persons sometimes change their minds about moral beliefs. At one point in time a person may believe that abortions are morally wrong. If that person comes to believe that abortions are morally acceptable, it appears that a moral judgment that was once right is no longer right. If relativists claim to have good reasons for changing their minds, then they would have to maintain that their earlier judgment was, in fact, wrong. Individual ethical relativism seems to maintain that the *mere holding* of a belief is justifying grounds for calling it a *right* belief. This would seem an absurd approach to defending a moral conviction.

Similar *reductio* arguments can be made against cultural ethical relativism. According to the cultural ethical relativist, a culture that holds slaves is morally equal to a culture that rejects slavery. Or, as in the case of an old Hindu tradition, the burning alive of a widow on the funeral pyre of her husband (*sati*) was, in fact, morally appropriate. *Sati* is against the law in modern India, so it is no longer morally acceptable in that culture. It seems absurd to maintain that what is now no longer morally acceptable was once truly morally acceptable.

A related *reductio* argument holds that cultural ethical relativism makes moral progress—or moral decline—impossible. A culture that changes its mind about *sati* has not improved its moral status. It merely holds a different view about *sati*. Furthermore, active moral reformers in a culture would in principle be mistaken in their efforts since such efforts at reform involve a rejection of the moral views currently held by that culture. An anti-slavery reformer would be mistaken in claiming that the current slave-holding culture was morally mistaken. These various implications of cultural ethical relativism would appear to reveal the absurdity of that theory.

A persevering ethical relativist might respond that while ethical relativism does entail the results which are labeled as "absurd," those entailments are *not* absurd but can be affirmed. There is neither moral improvement nor moral decline. A Hitler is the moral equal of the Buddha or Saint Francis. This response would grate against the moral intuitions that most of us hold. It does seem clear that the power of these *reductio* arguments hinges largely on the moral intuitions we hold. This would require us to defend these intuitions in some way. These defenses are explored in Chapters 6 and 7.

Ethical Relativist as Closet Egoist

Another argument against ethical relativism consists in the attempt to show that the ethical relativist, when unmasked, is really an ethical egoist. For instance, persons may be initially attracted to ethical relativism since it appears to provide a way of escaping from the demands of commonly held moral values. Ethical egoism is one formulation of an absolutist position.[127]

The purported individual ethical relativist claims, "What I believe to be right is right for me, and what you believe to be right is right for you. Such is the good old American individualistic tradition." However, if the arguments against ethical relativism given above are at all cogent, then such a claim seems basically incoherent. Thus, what the relativist probably intends to assert is something like "After all, I want to do what I think is best for myself, and others can do what they believe is best for them." That would be a coherent position but would be an expression of ethical egoism which is an absolutist claim: "The morally correct action is that action which results in advantage to oneself." Epicurus defended this view centuries ago, and it has contemporary advocates. It is, however, a form of ethical absolutism, not ethical relativism. The ethical relativist is exposed as a closet egoist. Ethical egoism, at least, has a long tradition of support by a variety of philosophers.

Chapter 4 of this work reviewed a series of ethical theories which were absolutist in nature. There were considerable disagreements about the *nature* of that absolute, but all of them rejected ethical relativism. This chapter has also expressed opposition to ethical relativism. Furthermore, Chapter 7 of this work defended a form of ethical absolutism by advocating the theory of *rational egoism* which has been expressed by a variety of thinkers—religious and non-religious. In review, rational egoism maintains that the primary moral principle is the pursuit of the long-range goal of personal fulfillment. Of course, the very idea of what constitutes "fulfillment" varies among philosophers. Rational egoism is, however, not a call for selfishness since our long-range pathway to fulfillment would naturally involve others that we love and care about. Their fulfillment constitutes an element of our fulfillment. This chapter leaves us with an open question: What, in fact, is the best pathway to a truly fulfilling life?

9

The Free Will Problem

I do not believe in free will. . . . This awareness of the lack of free will keeps me from taking myself and my fellow men too seriously as acting and deciding individuals, and from losing my temper.

—Albert Einstein[128]

You say: I am not free. But I have raised and lowered my arm. Everyone understands that this illogical answer is an irrefutable proof of freedom.

—Leo Tolstoy[129]

Consider the following scenarios: 1) Your car refuses to start on a cold winter morning. You probably would not hold it *morally responsible* for that failure. It did not *intend* to act up in that way and could not *have done otherwise* under the circumstances. However, you would no doubt look for the reason and then do something to *alter the future behavior* of said car. 2) Your dog tore up the living room sofa during your absence. Did the dog *intend* to do that? Could the dog have *done otherwise* given the circumstances? Do you hold the dog *morally responsible* for those actions? You would probably do something to *alter the dog's future behavior*. 3) A member of your community robbed a local bank. Did the robber *intend* to do it? Under the circumstances, could the robber have *done otherwise?* Would you hold that person to be *morally responsible* for that action? Would you seek to do something that would *alter the future behavior* of that robber?

Those scenarios set up the problem of free will, determinism, and moral responsibility. While we would not hold either the car or the dog morally responsible, it would seem natural for us to hold the robber morally responsible for the action, Why do we hold the person morally responsible but neither the auto nor the dog? This issue has been debated for thousands of years by philosophers and theologians. Three major theories which provide answers to this question have been offered: 1) Free Will Theory, 2) Hard Determinism, and 3) Soft Determinism.

Some Definitions

The *Free Will Theory* holds that human beings have free will and can, therefore, be held morally responsible for deliberate actions. The robber had free will and could have done otherwise; therefore, we hold him morally responsible. We can justify punishing the robber for that action. This punishment is seen as deserved. Cars and dogs do not have free will and thus could not have done otherwise. They cannot be held morally responsible and do not justly deserve punishment.

The *Hard Determinist Theory* claims that human beings do not have free will and cannot be held morally responsible. Human beings do not have free will because *all* events in the universe—including moral choices—are necessarily *caused* by antecedent circumstances. Neither the car nor the dog have free will and could not have done otherwise; therefore, we do not hold either morally responsible. Given the truth of determinism, the robber did not have free will and could not have done otherwise. Therefore, the robber cannot be held morally responsible and does not justly deserve punishment. However, we are justified in attempting to do something to alter the future behavior of the robber.

The *Soft Determinist Theory* holds that human beings do not have free will but persons can still be held morally responsible. Soft Determinists agree with the Hard Determinists that all events in the universe—including moral choices—are caused by antecedent circumstances. Cars, dogs, and human beings do not have free will. The robber could not have done otherwise since his actions were caused. Nevertheless, we are properly concerned about the future behavior of the robber, so we seek appropriate ways to alter the robber's future behavior. By carrying out some methods of altering the robber's future behavior by reward or punishment, we are, in effect, holding him morally responsible.

Crucial factors in this debate include the theory of universal determinism, the theory of free will, and the concept of moral responsibility. *Universal determinism* holds that all events in the universe—including human choices—are necessarily caused by antecedent circumstances. The *free will theory* maintains that some human choices are not entirely caused by antecedent circumstances and that we can freely choose among possible actions. *Moral responsibility* is assigned when a person commits an immoral act and is properly punished for that act, or when a person performs a morally praiseworthy action and is justly rewarded for that action.

In Support of Determinism

There are a variety of arguments in support of universal determinism. 1) We instinctively look for causes that result in some event. How did that fire begin? Why did that person die? Why does an apple fall *down* from a tree instead of *up*? Most of us would not raise that last question, although tradition holds that Isaac Newton did raise that question in the process of developing the theory (law) of gravity. 2) It would seem most odd to claim that some event did *not* have a cause. If someone asks of a small boy who is holding a slingshot why that vase was broken, the answer "Nothing caused it, it just happened" would not be accepted. 3) When we want to accomplish some end or goal, we exert some action that we assume will be a *cause* for that end or goal. Without such an assumption, few ends or goals would be pursued. 4) We come to discover or learn that certain specific actions bring about certain results. We count on this regularity everyday of our lives. 5) Universal determinism is generally assumed in all scientific enterprises. Scientists look for causes in order to explain certain facts. It is this assumption that sustains scientists as they seek to understand the world of nature. Furthermore, this assumption has been enormously fruitful as science achieves a greater understanding of the world of nature as well as how to manipulate nature toward our own ends. 6) We generally look upon *reasons* as *causes*. If Joe gives you a reason (R) for why he did X, we accept his "reason" as a *causal* explanation of why he did what he did. Joe did X *because* of R.

In Support of Free Will

A preliminary clarification is required. The free will issue is sometimes confused because of a failure to make a distinction between freedom of *action* and freedom of the *will*. We have *freedom of action* whenever we are not restrained or limited in some way and are able to do certain actions. Most of our actions and choices illustrate this freedom. We are not "free" to leap over ten-story buildings because of our own limitations. If incarcerated, we are not free to pursue many things we would want to pursue. If chained to a wall, we are not free to move about. All three of the theories presented agree that we often have this freedom of action.

Freedom of the will is a more subtle concept. To have freedom of the will is to have the ability to choose among a variety of options at any one point in time. For instance, at Fast Food Inc., Joe is able to freely choose between a hot dog and a burger. Determinists deny this freedom. Determinists maintain that at any point in time Joe's next choice or action is totally caused by antecedent events or conditions in his life. At Fast Food Inc., his choice of either the hot dog or the burger is totally shaped by such circumstances. He chose the hot dog, for instance, because he could not have done otherwise.

A variety of arguments have been given in support of the Free Will Theory. The most compelling argument may arise from our own experience. We *feel* that we have this freedom when we take an action or make a decision. While he himself was a determinist, Tolstoy offers this point in the epigraph of this chapter as he speaks for our consciousness of freedom. When we raise an arm, we *feel* that we freely chose to do so and could have done otherwise. We freely *willed* the action. We do not feel that we were compelled to raise the arm because of antecedent circumstances. Given our own experience of freely choosing an action, we assume that others have the same experience and demonstrate the same freedom of the will. The Free Will Theory grants that there may be times when we did not act out of free will—as when we are startled and jump at the sound of a loud noise. Deliberate actions, however, are freely willed.

Another argument offered is a reformulation of the one just given. Our basic inclination to reward or to punish others for certain actions implies that we believe they had freedom of the will and could have done otherwise. This inclination seems deeply rooted in our psychological makeup and has been expressed by human beings in every culture and many religious traditions. How could an eternal Hell be rationally justified if sinners did not have freedom of the will? If we believed that such persons could not help but do what they did—that their actions were caused—we would not feel that we could justify reward or punishment. This basic urge to punish or reward is grounded in the belief in free will. Persons ought to be held morally responsible. How else could a penal system be justified?

Some argue that serious scientific research and inquiry presupposes freedom of the will. In doing research, the scientist reflects on a variety of possible theories and methods of confirmation of such theories. In doing so, scientists appear to assume that the choices made during research were freely made on the basis of a range of considered evidence. Could the scientist take the scientific method and its results seriously if they believed that they could not have done otherwise—that their methods and results were totally caused by antecedent circumstances? This argument has a certain air of paradox: scientists assume universal determinism as they seek data and theory confirmation; yet scientists believe that they exercise an element of freedom in doing the research and in reaching conclusions.

Determinist Rebuttal

In rebuttal, the Determinist would hold that the mere "feeling" of free will is not sufficient evidence to lead to the conclusion that we actually *have* free will. The family dog may feel as if it has free will. Do robots feel that they have free will? Consider the computer, HAL 9000, in *2001: A Space Odyssey*. The commander in *Space Odyssey* felt compelled to alter the future behavior of HAL 9000.

The Determinists would grant that human history reveals that most human beings and cultures believed that persons should be rewarded or punished for their actions because they had free will and should be held accountable. However, the Determinists could argue that this only demonstrates the long history of human error. We have largely rejected the theory of witches and that the earth is the center of the solar system. Even so, modern knowledge and the success of science lead to the rejection of the theory of free will.

Determinists could also note that not all religious traditions affirm that human beings have freedom of the will. Some have held that human beings are in bondage to their corrupt heart and are unable to freely choose the good. The question of the justification of an eternal Hell remains: Augustine, Aquinas, Luther, and Calvin—among others—wrestled with this problem. Furthermore, many determinists have rejected the concept of an eternal Hell as well as the religious beliefs related to that concept.

Finally, Determinists argue that the very idea of a "free will" fails under examination. In what sense can our "will" be free from antecedent circumstances? "Will" is not a *name* for some kind of human faculty; it is a way of referring to the process of choice-making. In analyzing this choice-making process it becomes clear that our choices are influenced by a great variety of events, experiences, beliefs, and characteristics. As human beings, we are shaped largely by the cultures into which we were inducted. The very aim of induction and tradition is to shape us so that we *will* act in certain ways. While a tradition may also assume free will, it also recognizes that the will can be shaped—if not compelled—in a variety of ways by way of reward and punishment. Books offering advice on child-raising seem to assume that parental actions can *cause* certain behaviors of their children. Without that assumption, the advice would seem empty.

The determinist maintains that our choices and actions are caused by antecedent circumstances. These circumstances include a vast array of factors: our genetic heritage, our education and beliefs, our tastes and preferences, our hopes and fears. Our choices and actions can be thought of as being "multi-causal" in nature; probably no one factor controls the causal stream. When Joe chose a hot dog instead of a burger at Fast Food Inc., a variety of factors caused that choice, according to the determinist: taste preference, a price special, a yen for a variety in his diet, what his friend may have ordered. What role could a fictional "free will" play in that choice? If free will refers to an uncaused choice—a choice free of all antecedent circumstances—it seems difficult to understand just what would prompt the free will to so freely choose. A choice disconnected from all antecedent circumstances would have no grounding at all in our life processes.

On Holding Persons Morally Responsible

The Free Will Theory is clear regarding moral responsibility. We have free will; we deliberately chose to act in that manner; we could have done otherwise. Therefore, if the act was morally reprehensible, the actor deserves punishment. If the act was morally praiseworthy, the actor deserves praise or reward.

The Hard Determinist position is also clear. Since all events are caused, our choices and actions are caused. We could not have done otherwise. Therefore, we cannot hold persons morally responsible. Neither praise nor blame is an appropriate response to some morally significant action. However, this does not imply that we have no proper response or recourse when someone perpetrates a deed of which we disapprove. We are not rationally obligated to pat the felon on the head, say that we understand he could not have done otherwise, and let him go his way. We will want to alter the future behavior of that person by warnings, fines, imprisonment, or some other form of behavior modification.

The Soft Determinist echoes most of the position taken by the Hard Determinist: all events are caused, including human choices. Nevertheless, we can hold persons morally responsible. We do this by seeking to alter the future behavior of that person by some means of reward or sanction. What the Soft Determinist *means* by "holding persons morally responsible" is that we are justified in seeking to alter the future behavior of someone by some means of behavior modification.

Implications Regarding Penal Systems

The three theories that have been explored have implications regarding law enforcement and criminal prosecution. What, for instance, is the justification of imprisonment for some defined crime? The Free Will Theory could claim that such imprisonment is a properly deserved *punishment* for the crime committed. This is punishment viewed as *retribution*—as somehow righting the scales of good and evil in the world. However, for the Free Will theorist, such punishment would not be seen as a means of altering the future behavior of the felon. Since the will of the felon is free from a causal sequence, it will not necessarily be altered by some attempt on our part to *cause* different behavior.

Neither Determinist could support the view of punishment as *retribution*—as balancing the scales of good and evil. Instead, both determinists would see punishment or reward as *therapy*—as a means of helping to correct the behavior of the person in mind. Since the person could not have done otherwise, punishment as *retribution* would be pointless and cruel. Prison systems should be set up for the purpose of rehabilitation, not vindictive punishment. This view does raise the question of capital punishment. The death penalty seems based on some view of punishment as retribution—as some form of balancing the scales of good and evil, as some form of "getting even." On the other hand, the death penalty is certainly a means of altering future behavior in its most radical form. Could a Determinist consent to the death penalty of one person as a means of altering the future behavior of *other* potential felons? I leave that as an open question.

Some Puzzles

A student's question: "Professor, why do you believe that determinism is true?" Professor's answer: "I couldn't help it." Determinists believe that all events, including human choices, are caused by antecedent circumstances. This would imply that the position taken by the Determinist was the result of a causal chain. The Determinist's belief that Determinism is true was itself caused. The Determinist could not have done otherwise. This being the case, does the Determinist have any grounds for claiming the adequacy—or "truth"—of determinism? I leave that as an open question.

The Soft Determinist Theory does appear to carry an implication that seems to run counter to our intuitions. If "holding someone morally responsible" means "altering future behavior by various sanctions," then it appears that we hold our dogs to be "morally responsible" when we seek to alter the dog's future behavior. Some Soft Determinists appear willing to accept that implication.

10

Evolution and Ethics

> Ultimately our moral sense or conscience becomes a highly complex sentiment—originating in the social instincts, largely guided by the approbation of our fellow-men, ruled by self-reason, and confirmed by instruction and habit.
>
> —Charles Darwin[130]

> Biologists do not have special abilities to assess what is ethical;... there are within biology no magic solutions to moral problems.
>
> —Richard Alexander[131]

William James's analysis of morality, explored in Chapter 2, concluded that the point of moral philosophy is that of discovering the appropriate way of arbitrating among the conflicting wants, needs, and desires (WNDs) of sentient creatures. According to that analysis, our current moral setting involves almost eight billion human beings and multitudes of other sentient creatures, each with wants, needs, and desires. Certainly not all of these can be honored; hence, some must go unfulfilled. This current moral setting, with its struggle of need against need and creature against creature, is parallel to the scene reflected in theories proposed by the Reverend Thomas Malthus (1776–1834), English economist and philosopher. He concluded that the ability of the human species to reproduce its kind would, if not restricted in some way, lead to a growth in population that would far exceed the resources needed to sustain it. There would be, as Malthus put it, a "struggle for existence." The gap between population demands and available resources seemed inevitable unless population increase was somehow limited. This limitation, Malthus observed, would come about by way of premature death through disease, starvation, and war as well as attempts to check the birth rate. Since the latter seemed ineffective, it was left largely for early death to keep population in check.

While Malthus maintained this pessimistic view of the human scene, he worked out a way of fitting his theory into the structure of his own religious faith, which was not strictly orthodox at all points. Even though he suffered some abuse by those more optimistic about the scheme of things, his theories did attract the attention of others. The most significant impact make by Malthus on future thought was through his influence on Charles Darwin (1809–82), whose theory of evolution through natural selection was prompted, in part, by the Malthusian description of the "struggle for existence."

Enter Charles Darwin

In *Darwin's Dangerous Idea*, Daniel Dennett confesses that he would give Charles Darwin an award for "the single best idea anyone has ever had." The idea of evolution by natural selection is "not just a wonderful idea. It is a dangerous idea."[132] However Darwin's idea might be rated, there is little doubt that his theory of evolution has had an immense impact on many sciences. It also has the marks of a very successful scientific theory. Great scientific theories are marked, for instance, by their ability to unify many fields of learning. "In a single stroke, the idea of evolution by natural selection unifies the realm of life, meaning, and purpose with the realm of space and time, cause and effect, mechanism and physical law."[133]

Great scientific theories also have explanatory power. The aim of any scientific theory, after all, is that of explaining observed phenomena in some way. (Newton's theory of gravitation explained, for instance, why an apple falls *down* from the tree.) While Darwin aimed primarily at explaining just how various species came into being, his theory now encompasses many other aspects of animal and human life. A variety of questions, including the following, have been explained by evolutionary theory. Why do males in many species develop tusks, fangs, horns, and other weapons? Why, in many species, do only a few males do most of the copulating? What accounts for acts of infanticide on the part of males (lions, chimpanzees, human beings)? Why do females, in most bird and mammalian species, tend to make a larger "parental investment" in their offspring than the males by giving more time and energy to raising their children? Why have human societies moved largely to monogamous marriages—at least in terms of legal patterns?

Evolution Encounters Morality

For several decades, biologists and philosophers have expanded the explanatory range of Darwin's theory by seeking to apply it to morality. Evolutionary theory has been used to explain just why human beings have developed and expressed patterns of behavior that reflect moral issues: violence of all kinds, selfishness, kindness, altruistic behavior, cooperation, cheating, truth-telling, lying, mating, rules of sexual conduct, and schemes of justice and fairness? The literature is both fascinating and abundant.[134]

Central issues in the various discussions include: 1) Can morality be reduced, ultimately, to biological facts so that biology can not only *explain* but also *justify* moral patterns? 2) To what extent can cultural patterns and belief systems—as religions—alter behavioral tendencies rooted in biological heritage? 3) If biology cannot fully explain and justify moral patterns, can it provide insight for those who attempt to construct or enforce moral patterns? The old question of "nature vs. nurture" is clearly involved, and the answers given by writers vary within the nature/nurture spectrum. Edward O. Wilson emphasizes the nature component:

> The genes hold culture on a leash. The leash is very long, but inevitably values will be constrained in accordance with their effects on the human gene pool. The brain is a product of evolution Human behavior—like the deepest capacities for emotional responses which drive and guide it—is the circuitous technique by which human genetic material has been and will be kept intact.[135]

While Michael Ruse makes a striking claim:

> In an important sense, ethics as we understand it is an illusion fobbed off on us by our genes to get us to cooperate.... Furthermore, the way our biology enforces its ends is by making us think that there is an objective higher code, to which we are all subject.[136]

R. D. Alexander, while deeply impressed by the power of biological heritage, suggests that nurture through culture has a creative role to play in constructing moral values:

> We are thus evolved to be nepotists, even though, because of the role of social learning and the nature of consciousness, purpose, and deliberation, we are not obliged to be nepotists.[137]

I will not engage directly in the nature/nurture debate. Instead, I will outline conclusions generally established by biologists and philosophers about how evolution has shaped values and behavior and then explore the relationship of these conclusions to moral theory.

A clarification needs to be made about various terms that will be used in the following pages such as "intention," "designed," "strategy," "selfish," and "altruistic." When these terms are applied to the processes or results of evolution, they are meant to be understood metaphorically. Biologists presently agree that no entity as "evolution" exists that can do anything like intend, design, etc. Furthermore, most biologists quoted also generally believe that there is no mind or consciousness within, under, or beyond nature that does the designing or has certain intentions. There is no God behind the scene. Instead, evolution is a name for a process reflected in nature that explains many phenomena of the natural world. Evolution, itself, is taken as a "brute fact" that cannot be explained in terms of some other theory or supposition.

As a theory, evolution began as an explanation of how various forms of plant and animal life have developed out of simple early forms of life. Darwin's major contribution was that of showing how *natural selection* could account for the development of various species, including human beings, from simpler forms of life. The focus in his major work was on physiological characteristics and how they developed and changed over time. In the latter part of the twentieth century, sociobiology and evolutionary psychology were developed and explored. Scientists who initiated this research reasoned that evolution could not only explain the physiological development of creatures, but could also explain their social behavior. If the genetic constitution of creatures shapes the physical characteristics of bees, rats, apes, and human beings, so also could genetic material tend to control the individual and social behavior of these various creatures. The results of this research have been impressive.[138]

Enter: The Selfish Gene

Evolutionary psychology and sociobiology have established a number of widely accepted conclusions. I will develop these conclusions, in no particular order of importance, and then examine the relationships between these conclusions and morality. A major advance in evolutionary theory was clearly expressed by Richard Dawkins in *The Selfish Gene*.[139] The major idea in that book is that organisms, such as human beings, are not the central actors in the evolutionary process. Instead, genes—molecules of DNA—are the basic units of natural selection. Organisms have their place in the process since they can be seen as "gene machines" that help to propagate, not the organism itself, but various genes carried by that organism. My own body, for instance, does not and cannot replicate itself; but it can, with the help of another body of the opposite sex, function to replicate some of my genes. My child will carry copies of half of my own genes. A "successful" organism, from this point of view, is one that maximizes the number of copies of its genes that are passed on. These genes survive in other organisms, but the present organism dies. These genes are "selfish" in the sense that they seek their own welfare at the cost of the organism that functions as the gene machine, and often at the cost of other genes as well. Cancer, for instance, can be thought of as rebellious cells shaped by rebellious genes that seek to replicate themselves but at great cost to the organism they inhabit. Paradoxically, if these cancer cells are too "successful," they finally bring about their own demise by ending the life of the host body. Truly successful genes are those that inhabit organisms that have the capacity to pass the genes on through reproduction.

From the "selfish gene" perspective, evolutionary theory is entirely compatible with the common sense notion that the individual is dispensable in evolutionary terms. Species and genes tend to be preserved, but the individual creature ultimately faces certain death—with the possible exception of some simple creatures such as amoebas that can, in theory, keep on dividing and avoid individual death.

On the other hand, the individual is important as a link to the next generation and as a means of passing on a genetic pattern. Genes, if they are to replicate, require gene machines that have the capacity to do the replicating. Hence, the individual must survive long enough to bring in the next generation. The fear of death or the fear of being attacked would be a genetic trait that could help an individual to survive long enough to propagate its kind. An individual or a species without such a fear would have little chance of surviving in the contest for life. Spiders, perhaps, do not *experience* a fear of death, and they may not even *experience* a fear of being attacked. Nevertheless, they have inherited through their genes various strategies that help them to avoid and escape from danger. Human beings, on the other hand, not only have a *fear* of being attacked, but they also have a fear of dying—a fear that may be peculiar to the human species. Animals die, but human beings come to realize that they *will* die. This realization usually becomes clear when a child is around ten years of age. One scholar argues that this fear of death shapes much of human activity.[140]

Evolution and Selfishness

Another feature of human beings that contributes to the survival of the individual in the early months of life is selfishness—a behavior encoded in our genes. Richard Dawkins notes that "we are born selfish."[141] One might object that it seems unfair to label a baby as "selfish," but Dawkins uses the word in a behavioral sense and not as a psychological term describing a motive. Thus, for Dawkins, babies *act* in selfish ways—especially during the early months of life—in that they seem not at all concerned about the needs of others but insist on expressing their own needs. This is what we have come to expect of babies, and their behavior no doubt helps them to survive. Parents often agree that it is fortunate that babies are "cute" since it would be difficult to tolerate their demands if they were not.

This selfish behavior is displayed in most animal species. In a litter of pigs, for instance, there is considerable competition for milk from the mother. If the litter is large, a smaller and weaker piglet may not survive. Such a death would allow more food for the remaining siblings leaving them stronger and better able to replicate their genes. In bird species, competition for food from the parents is also intense. The baby bird with the loudest cry and conspicuous mouth is most apt to get fed. There is some evolutionary wisdom in that scene since feeding the strong is an advantage to the genetic line. In a tragic parallel, mothers in poverty-stricken settings sometimes must decide which child will get the food needed for life. She must use her meager resources to help the stronger children thereby allowing the weaker to die. The most striking example of "selfishness" in some bird species is a type of fratricide wherein baby birds will eject other eggs from the nest before they hatch. The female in some bird species will lay her eggs in a "foster" bird's nest where the resulting chick will destroy other eggs or hatchlings. This picture is not pleasant, but it does display another means for a species to survive and replicate its genes.[142]

Evolution and Sympathy

Selfishness is not the entire story, however, since in the long run pure selfishness will not succeed. In the human species, parents are often gratified to notice that children do develop a sense of sympathy. In many species it is common for individuals to exhibit "altruistic" actions in the sense they these actions benefit other individuals without any immediate benefit to the altruist. For instance, in some monkey and bird species, an individual may give a warning cry as a sign of danger so that others might take cover. The warning cry itself may even increase the danger to the one giving the cry since a predator would more easily identify the presence of that individual.

This altruism is difficult to understand in traditional evolutionary theory since it appears to work against the survival of the altruistic individual. This altruism is more easily explained by evolutionary psychology with its focus on the "selfish gene" since altruism may enhance the reproductive success of the genes *shared* by the monkey or the bird, even though it may reduce the survival chances of the altruist. These actions are understood in terms of kin selection altruism and/or reciprocal altruism, both of which have the advantage of maximizing the reproduction of genes even at some cost to an individual.

Kin Selection Altruism

The concepts of *kin selection altruism* and *reciprocal altruism* require a brief description. Kin selection altruism occurs when altruistic actions—such as sharing food with a related individual—take place only with a relative, not with a non-related individual. Related lions in the same pride will share food with each other as long as there is enough food to go around. When food is scarce, the adult lions will eat the kill before the cubs have a chance to eat. This makes survival sense, since if the adults die, the cubs cannot survive. If the cubs die but the adults survive, more cubs can be produced.

A lion with genes for purely altruistic acts may not survive. Consider: If a lion with purely altruistic genes gave handouts to lions from other prides when food was scarce, that action would work to the disadvantage of the altruist and its genes. In the competition for food, that lion would not survive. Hence, we would expect that altruistic gene to be eliminated from the population. Since lions of the same pride share genes, their kin altruism is an advantage for the pride and, hence, for the successful replication of their shared genes. This point is clearly illustrated in many species, including human beings. We are much more apt to share our resources with those closely related to us than with those completely unrelated. In general, we are more inclined to share our resources with our children, who share half of our genes, than with a cousin who shares a smaller fraction. Such kin selection altruism helps maximize the replication of our genes.

Reciprocal Altruism

Reciprocal altruism takes place when individuals share resources with others, at some cost to themselves, even when the others are not related. Such altruistic actions make evolutionary sense only if these actions help ensure that the recipient will someday repay the altruist in kind and thus enable the altruist to maximize its genetic replication. If an altruist gave away resources to just anyone without any hope that it would some day be returned, the altruist would find it hard to survive and its undiscriminating genes would be eliminated. She would be "too good for her own good." Such an altruist would be a "sucker" in evolutionary terms. I may, for instance, be willing to help my unrelated neighbor; but if I continue to do so and he never reciprocates, I am very apt to stop helping that neighbor. If I continued to help, I would be classified as a sucker. But if my altruistic actions are reciprocated and I am helped in return, then I may better prosper, and the chances of maximizing my genetic replication would be enhanced. "If you scratch my back, I'll scratch yours."

Employers and employees regularly illustrate such reciprocal altruism, even though the tradeoffs may not be entirely equal. Vampire bats are known to regurgitate blood in order to feed a neighbor back in the cave who failed to feed that night. This saves the neighbor from starving. However, the starving bat will get such help only from a bat who recognizes that it has been helped by the needy bat on an earlier occasion. Others refuse to supply the food. This bat behavior is clearly a case of mutual back scratching. Whether or not such reciprocal altruism is *truly* altruistic is a question that has generated considerable discussion.[143] Indeed, truly altruistic self-sacrificing actions can be seen as evolutionary mistakes.[144] If altruism is understood in terms of psychological motive or intention, then the word does not apply to insects and probably not to most animal species. While kin selection and reciprocal altruism are demonstrated among human beings, both reflect what David Hume called "confined generosity."

Evolution and Enemies

If evolutionary psychology explains various forms of altruistic behavior in terms of kin selection and reciprocal altruism with their related qualities (goodwill, humility, faith, hope, charity), then it should also be able to explain the darker side of human and animal nature (envy, deceit, hatred, anger, enmity). This, of course, can be done by the same appeal to the selfish gene theory. In a world where resources are often limited, the organisms that most successfully maximize their genes are those that can defend themselves against enemies of various kinds. For human beings, two kinds of enemies are confronted. First there are those enemies that use human flesh for their own nourishment—various large carnivores and omnivores, as well as bacteria and virus. We have largely overcome the danger from carnivores and omnivores and are fighting a continuing battle against our smaller enemies.

The second enemy we confront is other human beings—those within our own societies and those we consider to be enemy nations or groups. Human beings without some genetic capacity for deceit, hate, anger, and ferocity would certainly lose their competitive advantage in the race for genetic replication.

Group Selection

It seems, then, that any group struggling for survival would have its chances enhanced by practicing kin selection and reciprocal altruism within the group while expressing various forms of enmity toward competing groups. If individuals with genes that support behavior such as kin selection and reciprocal altruism are survivors, it would suggest that that these genes would be deeply imbedded in the group itself. Thus groups of creatures, such as human beings, may take on these tactics. Tribal loyalty, for instance, would become significant in a tribe as individuals with genes that foster tribal loyalty become dominant. Individuals lacking such "loyalist" genes would have a tendency to drop away from a tribe either by choice or by ostracism or outright banishment. On the other hand, if a tribe develops a sufficient number of tribe-supporting altruists—call them "patriots"—that tribe will have numbers willing to die for the tribe/nation thus enhancing the flourishing of the tribe. While some biologist/philosophers challenge the concept of group selection, Elliot Sober and D. H. Wilson defend it.[145]

Evolution appears to have produced various forms of tribalism with human tribes of nation, religion, and race, resulting in disastrous forms of the "struggle for existence" that Thomas Malthus once described. Most animal species will defend their territories or feeding grounds, but only human beings, with their special ingenuity, have learned how to wreak general havoc upon their enemies.

Evolution and Moral Advice

The question now to be examined is whether or not these tendencies developed through the evolutionary processes can give us any moral direction. If the genes we have inherited control the color of our eyes and skin as well as our height and intelligence, do they also make us selfish? Do the phenomena of kin selection and reciprocal altruism direct our moral decisions? Charles Darwin believed that a biological explanation can be given for humanity's moral proclivities:

> Any animal whatever, endowed with well-marked social instincts, the parental and filial affections being here included, would inevitably acquire a moral sense or conscience, as soon as its intellectual powers had become as well, or nearly as well developed, as in man.[146]

Biologist E. O. Wilson believes that "scientists and humanists should consider together the possibility that the time has come for ethics to be removed from hands of philosophers and biologized."[147] Granting that our moral proclivities may be rooted in our evolutionary heritage, the important question in current discussion is whether this heritage can tell us what we *ought* do. An examination of that question and related issues follows.

Most scientists and philosophers agree that while our genetic heritage may *incline* us toward certain actions and relationships, it does not *determine* our actions. They reject a completely biological deterministic view that would claim that our genetic heritage *alone* causes our behavior just as heritage causes the color of our eyes. This rejection reflects the view that nurture has an important role in modifying nature. Good parenting and good schools can make a difference. The socializing influences in our lives help shape our behavior. Just as a dog that may be inclined to jump onto the couch can be trained to remain on the floor, even so some patterns of a child's behavior—or adult's—can be altered through social processes such as education.

Psychological Egoism

The question of determinism raises the old issue of *psychological egoism*. This theory maintains that human beings are always motivated by what they believe to be in their self-interest. If this theory is true, then it would be impossible for a human being to choose to act in a purely altruistic way. A classic articulation of psychological egoism is found in Thomas Hobbes (1588–1679), who has been identified as the "first sociobiologist two hundred years before Darwin."[148] Hobbes claimed that all deliberate human actions are motivated by desires and that all human desires are self-interested. What we ultimately want is our own well-being, and all rational acts aim at that well-being. Even apparent acts of altruism were merely forms of disguised self-love. His theory, like all formulations of psychological egoism, is not a *normative* theory designed to show us how we *ought* to act; it is, rather, a psychological theory about human nature which seeks to explain just why persons act in the way they do. Later, the founders of utilitarianism, Jeremy Bentham and John Stuart Mill, both espoused a form of psychological egoism. *Ethical egoism*, on the other hand, differs from psychological egoism. Ethical egoism, as a normative theory, tells us we *ought* to pursue our own self-interests. As a descriptive theory, psychological egoism seeks to describe what *is* that case, not what *ought* to be the case.

A major difficulty in proving that psychological egoism is either true or false is that the theory is about motives, not about actions. Are all motives self-interested or selfish? It is difficult to discover what motives actually produce an action. Psychological egoism is certainly not a scientific theory that can be tested by way of empirical evidence. What kind of empirical evidence would count one way or another?

Some formulations of psychological egoism result in a theory that appears to be patently false. Joel Feinberg, for instance, defines psychological egoism as the theory that "all human actions when properly understood can be seen to be motivated by selfish desires."[149] While James Rachels has the psychological egoist claim that "Each person is so constituted that he will look out *only* for his own interests. . . . In the final analysis, we care nothing for other people."[150] If psychological egoism is formulated in such terms, then it is easily defeated for there are multitudes of counterexamples which show that such a theory must be false. A parent staying up all night to care for an ill child can hardly be accurately assessed as looking out "only for his own interests" or is "motivated by selfish desires." To be sure, the parent has his own interests, but he is also showing interest in the interests of the child. This is not "selfishness."

If psychological egoism is to have any credence, it must have a different formulation. I have proposed the following:

> Psychological egoism is the theory that all deliberate human actions involve a motive that is either self-regarding or, if other-regarding, involve a self-referential stimulus without which the action could not have taken place.[151]

More simply, psychological egoism is the theory that no deliberate action is purely altruistic; instead, all such actions are motivated by either a self-interested or self-referential element. The parent, for instance, may act out of concern for the sick child (not a "selfish" motive), but the action is clearly self-referential in that the child's well-being constitutes an important element in the parent's flourishing. While this formulation of psychological egoism cannot be conclusively proven to be true, it avoids the easy refutation of the formulations proposed by Feinberg and Rachels.[152] It is of some interest to note that my formulation of the theory is compatible with the categories of kin selection and reciprocal altruism espoused by theories of evolutionary psychology. Both behavioral patterns are clearly self-referential in terms of genetic interests.

David Hume: An Is-Ought Distinction

A major reason for claiming that evolution cannot give us any moral advice comes from the work of the eighteenth-century philosopher, David Hume. In his *A Treatise of Human Nature*, Hume argues that no empirical fact can, by itself, lead to some value claim or to some normative rule.[153] In short, he argues that no "is" can, by itself, yield an "ought." This is Hume's duly famous "is-ought distinction." For instance, the following are two statements of empirical fact: 1) A human fetus is a living entity. 2) A human fetus has the potential, under the right conditions, to develop into an adult human being. But these two statements of fact do not, by themselves, entail any type of normative claim such as "Abortion is morally wrong." (Note that the first statement does not claim that the fetus is a person. Even if it *did* make that assertion, no normative or moral claim could be logically derived from it.) In order to conclude "Abortion is morally wrong," from either statement, an additional premise that includes a moral judgment must be posited—such as 3) "It is wrong to kill a human fetus." Furthermore, premise 3 is not derived from any empirical fact but is, itself, a moral judgment usually derived from other non-empirical claims such as a theological assertion. Given Hume's point, it follows that no biological fact, by itself, can ever yield a moral assertion. It may be a biological fact that human beings have a genetic propensity to have sympathy for others, especially their kin. Nevertheless, that fact in itself does not yield the normative rule: "Have sympathy for others." Nor can the biological fact that human beings have some genetic propensity to kill those they see as dangers to themselves or their "tribe" entail the normative rule: "Kill your enemies." Moral judgments regarding sympathy or killing may be true or false—I leave that question open. But the truth or falsity of any such patterns do not stem from their evolutionary origins.

Genes vs. Beliefs

Finally, since beliefs can lead one to override a genetic predisposition, the role of nurture must be recognized. The choice of celibacy would be an example. Men and women of normal sexual drives elect to be celibate in a variety of religious traditions because of certain beliefs drawn from their traditions. From an evolutionary point of view, such celibacy would appear to be a mistake since it eliminates the possibility of replicating the celibate's genes. On the other hand, if one insists that the theory of evolution is a theory of (almost) everything, then one would propose some evolutionary strategy, even for celibacy. One possible theory would hold that such behavior by a small group of persons within a society might influence others by example. Such celibacy is usually accompanied by other forms of asceticism as a pledge to poverty, isolation from relatives, and an expressed compassion for all human beings and other creatures. These "saint" figures may, by example, influence others in that society to live a more generally altruistic life in relation to others in their community.

Among ordinary citizens, it may well be that we look for ways of encouraging just a bit more altruism in our neighbors than we, ourselves, would wish to express. Great saint figures may help us to encourage just such altruism in others. Furthermore, this caring within a community could certainly strengthen that community and enable it to survive in the face of attacks from others. Religions often provide a powerful bond in the believing community which can aid in that community's struggle against enemies. In this way, religions can have an evolutionary value for that community.

On the other hand, it can be argued that such behavior need not be explained in evolutionary terms. Evolutionary psychology, after all, suggests that evolutionary "strategy" is designed to maximize the replication of a gene pool and that self-sacrificing actions not designed to assist the family or clan would be a rejection of such strategy. There are some religious beliefs that show no interest whatsoever in extending a gene pool or maximizing genetic offspring in some form. These beliefs may run counter to what is deemed as evolutionary "success," but this, in itself, would not falsify such beliefs. The religions of India—Hinduism, Buddhism, and Jainism—have as their fundamental goal "release" from the endless round of rebirth or reincarnation. Maximizing their genetic offspring would have the unfortunate result of casting more "souls" into earthly suffering. Jainism expresses this view vividly in what appears to be a "rigorously world-denying" spiritual outlook.[154] The Jain saint is thoroughly ascetic, and great Jain saints escaped from embodied life by starving themselves to death. Their aim is to achieve release from embodied existence and find supreme bliss as a conscious soul at the top of the universe. Not all Jains (or Buddhists or Hindus) pursue this heroic spiritual pathway and, instead, marry and bring in the next generations. This enables such belief systems to stay off the endangered species list. A different fate faced the Shakers, a sect imported to the United States from England. They expected the return of Christ and also valued celibacy above marriage. After gaining a rather large number of adherents in the 1800s, the sect declined and as of 2019 there is only one active Shaker village remaining.

Another example of how beliefs could run counter to evolutionary "success" would be that of pacifism and the teachings to "love your enemies." The biologist-philosopher Sir Arthur Keith put the matter forcefully: "Christ annihilates the law of evolution, he throws a bomb right into the very heart of the machinery by which and through which nature has sought to build up races or breeds of mankind."[155] Pacifism and universal benevolence have been explained in evolutionary terms as adaptive behaviors among conquered or vulnerable people. For instance, Jesus lived when the Jews were under the heel of the Roman Empire which took no pity on those who resisted their rule. In that setting, cooperative and acquiescent behavior may be an effective survival strategy.[156]

Beliefs Trump Genetic Heritage

On the other hand, beliefs may trump evolutionary inclinations. If a theistic worldview is embraced, then pacifism, universal benevolence, and some forms of asceticism may be appropriate responses to such beliefs, and an evolutionary explanation need not be employed to account for such behavior. Whether or not such beliefs are true is quite another question. We need to remember, however, that such pacifism, universal benevolence, and asceticism are not viewed as self-sacrificing in the long run by those who pursue these practices on religious grounds. From within these belief systems, the promise of fulfillment for those who persevere is always there. A German Roman Catholic nun, working hard at cleaning guest facilities, put the matter succinctly: "Heaven is not cheap." The Muslim suicide bombers from radical Islamic sects evidently also saw such acts of devotion to be a means of immediate pathway to Heaven. These last two examples illustrate what Michael Ruse meant when he wrote, "Furthermore the way our biology enforces its ends is by making us think that there is an objective higher code, to which we all are subject."[157] Conflicting worldviews clearly stand behind many of these claims and arguments. Ruse would, evidently, not only explain the phenomena of religion in evolutionary terms but would also suggest that such explanations show religious beliefs, as such, to be false. This type of argument reflects the "genetic fallacy" in that Ruse appears to claim that the *origin* of an idea is grounds for rejecting the idea as false. As one would expect, other philosophers disagree with Ruse.[158]

While some beliefs may trump genetic heritage, there is strong evidence suggesting that some beliefs, themselves, are imbedded in our genetic heritage. In his *God is Watching You*, Dominic Johnson musters evidence from a variety of scientific fields suggesting that we carry within our psychological makeup a deep sense that we are being watched by some Divine Power.[159] This appears to be true even of those who claim to be atheists. Furthermore, Johnson's book demonstrates that this deep belief in something like Divine Eyes watching us does, in fact, considerably influence human behavior. Old gods may be hard to exorcise.

Endnotes

Introduction

1. Thompson, "Killing and Letting Die," 204–17.
2. Tillich, *Courage*, 51–54, for an analysis of types of guilt.

Chapter 1: A Theory about Moral Theories

3. Geertz, "Ethos," 326.
4. Hudson, *Modern*, 321.
5. Taylor, *Ethics*, xiii.
6. Mackie, *Ethics*, 232.
7. Harris, *End*, and *Moral*.
8. For an explanation of why systems of morality vary so much, see Johnson, "Explaining Diversity," 115–33.

Chapter 2: The Point of Morality

9. Alexander, *Biology*, 1.
10. Hudson, *Modern*, 326.
11. James, "Moral."
12. This view will be examined in Chapter 7.

Chapter 3: Beyond Morality: Meaning and Significance

13. Halverson, *Concise*, xiv. I am indebted to Halverson for much of this analysis.
14. Taylor, "Meaning."
15. Hemingway, *Complete*, 291.
16. Cited in Bellah, *Religion in Human Evolution*, 48.
17. Johnson, *Judging*, 1–9, for analyses of religious traditions as "The stories by which we live."
18. Newman, *Minister's*, 215.
19. Russell, "Free Man's," 61–62.

ENDNOTES

20. For a helpful introduction to Kierkegaard's thought, see Mullen, *Kierkegaard's Philosophy*.
21. Camus, *Fall*.
22. Data drawn from Paloutzian, *Invitation*.
23. Becker, *Escape*, 4.
24. Pascal, *Pensees and Other Writings*, 26, 73.
25. Tillich, *Courage*, 64–70, for a distinction between existential and neurotic anxiety.
26. Becker, *Denial*, ix.
27. Plato, *Phaedo*, 55.
28. Noss and Noss, *History*, 108.
29. 1 Cor 15:26.
30. Freud, *Future*, chapters 3 and 4.
31. See Bailey, *Greek Atomists*.
32. Lifton, *Life*.
33. Tillich, *Courage*, 51–54 for an analysis of the anxiety of guilt.
34. Noss and Noss, *History*, 103.
35. Becker, *Denial*, 5.

Chapter 4: Moral Theories and Worldviews

36. Tolstoy, "Religion and Morality," 31–32.
37. Taylor, *Ethics*, viii.
38. Stumpf, *Socrates to Sartre*, was a helpful source for this chapter.
39. *De Rarum Natura* (*On the Nature of Things*), by the Roman poet Titus Lucretius Carus (ca. 99–55 BCE) is a long Latin poem that celebrates and articulates the Epicurean worldview.
40. "Epicureanism became one of the dominant ethical creeds of antiquity." *Encyclopedia of Ethics*, 1:318.
41. Guthrie, *Greeks*, 364.
42. Thilly and Wood, *History*, 110.
43. A description of this "excellent man" is given in *Nicomachean Ethics* 4.
44. Barry, *Christian*, 93.
45. White, *Christian Ethics*, 100.
46. Matt 27:37–39.
47. Rom 13:10.
48. Aquinas, *Summa Theologica*, SMT SS Q[11] A [3] Body Para. ½.
49. Davies, *Thought*, 18.
50. Hume, "Enquiry," 689.
51. Hume, *Treatise* 4.3.3.
52. Stumpf, *Socrates*, 278.

ENDNOTES

53 Hume, *Philosophical*, IV, 246.
54 Baier, *David Hume*, vol. I, 569–70.
55 MacIntyre, *Short History*, 171.
56 Kant, *Grounding*, 3.
57 Thomas, *Religious*, 249.
58 Thomas, *Religious*, 250.
59 Bentham, *Introduction*, 791.
60 Bentham, *Introduction*, 793.
61 Leiter, *Death*, 386–402, supports Nietzsche's claim.

Chapter 5: Religion-based Morality

62 Geertz, "Ethos," 326.
63 Becker, *Encyclopedia of Ethics* for helpful survey essays on philosophical and religious ethics.
64 Whale, *Protestant*, 140–41.
65 White, *Christian Ethics*, for a review of Christian ethics. Noss and Noss, *History*, for a review of the ethics of non-Christian religions in the context of their own belief systems.
66 These descriptions are generalized sketches. The faiths offer highly nuanced interpretations.
67 Rom 13:10.
68 Kierkegaard, in *Stages*, and *Sickness*, explores the dynamics of the theological use of the Law.
69 Augustine, *Conf.* 2.4–10.
70 Tillich, *Systematic* 3:249–65.

Chapter 6: Self, Others, and Rights

71 James, "Remarks at the Peace Banquet," para. 2.
72 Sidgwick, *Methods*, 246.
73 See Singer, *Practical Ethics*, and Mackie, *Ethics*.
74 Bentham, "Introduction," 791.
75 Bellah, *Habits*, 282.
76 MacIntyre, *After Virtue*, 201. For an observation that links our various stories with religion and nationalism, see Alexander, *Biology*, 201–7.
77 Smart, *Beyond*, 227.
78 Smart, *Beyond*, 234.
79 Bellah, *Habits*, 56.
80 For example, see Juergensmeyer, *Terror*.
81 Gal 3:28.

82 Metzger and Murphy, *New Oxford*, 150.
83 White, *Christian Ethics*, 249-56.
84 White, *Christian Ethics*, 256.
85 See Juergensmeyer, *Terror*.
86 Krakauer, *Under the Banner*.
87 Juergensmeyer, *Terror*, 243.
88 Hobbes, "Leviathan," 163.
89 Ignatieff, *Human Rights*, xxv.
90 Lauren, *Evolution*, 20.
91 Lauren, *Evolution*, 19.
92 See Perry, *Idea*.
93 Orend, *Human Rights*, 87.
94 Mill, *Utilitarianism*, 52.
95 Orend, *Human*, 70. See, also, Rorty, *Philosophy*, 83-88.
96 Feinberg, *Social*, 94.

Chapter 7: Why Be Moral?

97 Ducasse, *Critical Examination*, 24.
98 MacIntyre, *After Virtue*, 67.
99 For extended analyses of the question "Why be moral?" see Green, *Religious Reason*, Chapters 2 and 3; and Singer, *Practical Ethics*, Chapter 3.
100 Green, *Religious Reason*, 20.
101 Hudson, *Modern*, 26.
102 Bentham, "Introduction," 791.
103 Taylor, *Ethics*, 108.
104 Frankena, *Ethics*, 19. Singer makes much the same point in his *Practical*, 10.
105 Mackie, *Ethics*, 190.
106 Gauthier, *Morality*, 438.
107 Baier, quoted in Gauthier, *Morality*, 438.
108 Singer, *Practical Ethics*, 10.
109 Frankena, *Ethics*, 113.
110 Frankena, *Thinking about Morality*, 87.
111 Frankena, *Thinking about Morality*, 91. Gert makes assertions that echo Frankena's position. "But although it is usually in a person's self-interest to be moral, it will sometimes not be so." Gert concedes that a philosophical understanding of morality is not enough. "It is also necessary for the natural compassion of humankind to be broadened and deepened. People must come to care for all other persons. . . . This is a task for art, literature, and religion." Gert, *Morality*, 341 and 386.
112 Baier, *Moral*, Chapter 5.
113 Singer, *Practical Ethics*, 317.

114 Hare, "Universalizability," 1258–61.
115 MacIntyre, *Whose Justice?*, 146ff.
116 Stumpf, *Socrates*, 111.
117 MacIntyre, *Whose Justice?*, 147.
118 MacIntyre, *Whose Justice?*, 148.
119 Cited in Johnson, *Judging*, 26.
120 Green, *Religion*.
121 Anscombe, "Modern Moral Philosophy."
122 Taylor, *Ethics*, 89–90.
123 Prothero, *American Jesus*, 30.
124 *Crimes and Misdemeanors*, an award-winning movie by Woody Allen, examined this theme.
125 Johnson, *God Is Watching You*.

Chapter 8: Ethical Relativism

126 James, "Moral Philosopher," 23.
127 Parks, *Critical Years*, for this argument.

Chapter 9: The Free Will Problem

128 White, *Einstein*, 262.
129 Tolstoy, *War and Peace*, 1336.

Chapter 10: Evolution and Ethics

130 Darwin, *Descent*, 500.
131 Alexander, *Biology*, xvi.
132 Dennett, *Darwin's Dangerous Idea*, 21.
133 Dennett, *Darwin's Dangerous Idea*, 21.
134 Major contributors would include, in alphabetical order: R. D. Alexander, R. Axelrod, Richard Dawkins, Daniel Dennett, Anthony Flew, Stephen Jay Gould, Holmes Rolston III, Michael Ruse, Peter Singer, R. L. Trivers, George C. Williams, D. S. Wilson, Edward O. Wilson.
135 Wilson, *On Human*, 167.
136 Ruse and Wilson, "Evolution of Ethics," 51. In Dennett, *Darwin's Dangerous Idea*, 470.
137 Alexander, *Biology*, 141.
138 See endnote 5, above, for a list of major contributors.
139 Dawkins, *Selfish Gene*.
140 For an impressive development of the fear of death and its consequences for human beings, see Becker, *Denial*.

ENDNOTES

141 Dawkins, *Selfish Gene*, 3.
142 Dawkins, *Selfish Gene*, 130–34.
143 See, for instance, Sober and Wilson, *Unto Others*.
144 Alexander, *Biology*, 191.
145 Sober, *Unto Others*.
146 Darwin, *Descent*, Chapter 4.
147 Wilson, *Sociobiology*, 27.
148 Dennett, *Darwin's Dangerous Idea*, 453.
149 Feinberg, "Psychological Egoism," 5.
150 Rachels, *Elements*, 53–54 (my emphasis).
151 Johnson, "Psychological Egoism," 243.
152 See Johnson, "Psychological Egoism," for an extended analysis of the issue.
153 Hume, *Treatise*, 469.
154 Noss and Noss, *History*, 94–104.
155 Keith, *Evolution*, 65.
156 Alexander, *Biology*, 176.
157 Ruse and Wilson, "Evolution of Ethics," 51.
158 For example, Rolston, *Genes*.
159 Johnson, *God Is Watching You*.

Bibliography

Alexander, Richard. *The Biology of Moral Systems*. New York: de Gruyter, 1987.
Anscombe, G. E. M. "Modern Moral Philosophy." In *The Is/Ought Question*, edited by W. D. Hudson, 175–95. London: Macmillan, 1967.
Aristotle. "Nicomachean Ethics." In *Classics of Western Philosophy*, edited by Stephen Cahn, 275–329. 4th ed. Indianapolis: Hackett, 1995.
Augustine. *The Confessions of St. Augustine*. Translated by F. J. Sheed. New York: Sheed and Ward, 1942.
Baier, Annette. "David Hume." In *Encyclopedia of Ethics* 1:565–77.
Baier, Kurt. *The Moral Point of View*. Ithaca, NY: Cornell University Press, 1958.
Bailey, C. *The Greek Atomists and Epicurus*. New York: Oxford University Press, 1928.
Barry, F. R. *Christian Ethics and Secular Society*. London: Hodder & Stoughton, 1966.
Becker, Ernest. *The Denial of Death*. New York: Free Press, 1973.
———. *Escape from Evil*. New York: Free Press, 1975.
Becker, Lawrence, ed. *Encyclopedia of Ethics*. New York: Garland, 1992.
Bellah, Robert. *Habits of the Heart*. Berkeley: University of California Press, 1985.
———. *Religion in Human Evolution*. Cambridge: Harvard University Press, 2011.
Bentham, Jeremy. "An Introduction to the Principles of Morality and Legislation." In *The English Philosophers from Bacon to Mill*, edited by E. A. Burt, 791–856. New York: Modern Library, 1939.
Berger, Peter. *The Sacred Canopy: Elements of a Sociological Theory of Religion*. Garden City, NY: Doubleday, 1967.
Berger, Peter, and Thomas Luckmann. *The Social Construction of Reality: A Treatise in the Sociology of Knowledge*. Garden City, NY: Doubleday, 1966.
Broad, C. D. "Egoism as a Theory of Human Motives." In *Egoism and Altruism*, edited by R. D. Milo, 88–100. Belmont, California: Wadsworth, 1973.
Brunner, Emil. *The Divine Imperative*. Translated by Olive Wyon. Philadelphia: Westminster, 1947.
Burt, Edwin A., ed. *The English Philosophers from Bacon to Mill*. New York: Modern Library, 1939.
Butler, Joseph. *Five Sermons*. New York: Bobbs-Merrill, 1950.
Cahn, Steven M., ed. *Classics of Western Philosophy*. 4th ed. Indianapolis: Hackett, 1995.
Cahn, S. and J. Haber, eds. *20th Century Ethical Theory*. Englewood Cliffs, NJ: Prentice Hall, 1970.

BIBLIOGRAPHY

Camus, Albert. *The Fall.* Translated by Justin Obrian. New York: Knopf, 1957.
Carmody, D. L., and J. T. Carmody. *How to Live Well: Ethics in the World Religions.* Belmont, CA: Wadsworth, 1988.
Darwin, Charles. *The Descent of Man and Selection in Relation to Sex.* New York: Appleton, 1871.
———. *On the Origin of Species.* 1st ed. Cambridge: Harvard University Press, 1964.
Davies, Brian. *The Thought of Thomas Aquinas.* Oxford: Clarendon, 1992.
Dawkins, Richard. *The Selfish Gene.* Oxford: Oxford University Press, 1976.
Dennett, Daniel. *Darwin's Dangerous Idea.* New York: Simon & Schuster, 1995.
Ducasse, C. J. *A Critical Examination of the Belief in Life after Death.* Springfield, IL: Thomas, 1961.
Feinberg, Joel. "Psychological Egoism." In *Moral Philosophy*, edited by George Sher, 5–15. New York: Harcourt Brace Jovanovich, 1987.
———. *Social Philosophy.* Englewood Cliffs, NJ: Prentice Hall, 1973.
Foot, Philippa. "Morality as a System of Hypothetical Imperatives." In *Virtues and Vices*, by Philippa Foot, 157–73. New York: Oxford University Press, 1978.
Frankena, William. *Ethics.* Englewood Cliffs, NJ: Prentice Hall, 1963.
———. *Thinking about Morality.* Ann Arbor, MI: University of Michigan Press, 1980.
Freud, Sigmund. *The Future of an Illusion.* New York: Anchor, 1964.
Gauthier, David. "Morality and Advantage." In *Twentieth Century Ethical Theory*, edited by S. Cahn and J. Haber, 437–46. Englewood Cliffs, NJ: Prentice Hall, 1970.
———. *Morality and Rational Self-Interest.* Englewood Cliffs, NJ: Prentice Hall, 1970.
———. *Morals by Agreement.* New York: Oxford University Press, 1986.
Gaylin, Willard. *Hatred: The Psychological Descent into Violence.* New York: Public Affairs, 2003.
Geertz, Clifford. "Ethos, World-view and the Analysis of Sacred Symbols." In *Man Makes Sense: A Reader in Modern Cultural Anthropology*, edited by E. Hammel and W. Simmons, 324–39. Boston: Little Brown, 1970.
———. "From Sine Qua Non to Cultural Systems." In *Ways of Understanding Religion*, edited by Walter Capps, 183–86. New York: Macmillan, 1972.
———. "Religion as a Cultural System." In *Reader in Comparative Religion: An Anthropological Approach*, edited by Lessa and Vogt, 167–76. New York: Harper & Row, 1958.
Gert, Bernard. *Morality: Its Nature and Justification.* Oxford: Oxford University Press, 2005.
Green, Ronald. *Religion and Moral Reason.* New York: Oxford University Press, 1988.
———. *Religious Reason.* New York: Oxford University Press, 1978.
Guthrie, W. K. C. *The Greeks and Their Gods.* Boston: Beacon, 1955.
Halverson, William. *A Concise Introduction to Philosophy.* 4th ed. New York: Random House, 1981.
Hammel, E., and W. Simmons. *Man Makes Sense: A Reader in Modern Cultural Anthrlopology.* Boston: Little Brown, 1970.
Hare, R. M. *Freedom and Reason.* Oxford: Oxford University Press, 1963.
———. *The Language of Morals.* New York: Oxford University Press, 1952.
———. *Moral Thinking.* Oxford: Oxford University Press, 1981.
———. "Universalizability." In *Encyclopedia of Ethics* 2:1258–61.
Harkness, Georgia. *The Sources of Western Morality.* New York: Scribner's, 1954

Harris, Sam. *The End of Faith; Religion, Terror, and the Future of Reason.* New York: Norton, 2004.

———. *The Moral Landscape: How Science Can Determine Human Values.* New York: Free Press, 2010.

Heil, John. *Rationality, Morality, and Self-Interest.* Lanham, MD: Rowman & Littlefield, 1993.

Hemingway, Ernest. *The Complete Short Stories of Ernest Hemingway.* New York: Scribner's, 1987.

Hobbes, Thomas. "Leviathan." In *The English Philosophers from Bacon to Mill,* edited by E. A. Burtt, 129–237. New York: The Modern Library, 1939.

Hudson, W. D. *The Is/Ought Question.* London: Macmillan, 1967.

———. *Modern Moral Philosophy.* Garden City, NY: Anchor, 1970.

Hume, David. *Dialogues Concerning Natural Religion.* Edited by N. K. Smith. New York: Social Science, 1948.

———. "An Enquiry Concerning Human Understanding." In *The English Philosophers from Bacon to Mill,* edited by E. A. Burtt, 585–689. New York: The Modern Library, 1939.

———. *The Philosophical Works of David Hume.* Edited by T. H. Green and T. H. Grose. 4 vols. London: Longman, Green, 1875.

———. *A Treatise on Human Nature.* Oxford: Clarendon, 1978.

Ignatieff, Michael. *Human Rights as Politics and Idolatry.* Princeton, NJ: Princeton University Press, 2001.

James, William. "The Moral Philosopher and the Moral Life." In *The Will to Believe and Other Essays in Popular Philosophy,* by William James, 184–215. New York: Dover, 1956.

———. *Pragmatism and the Meaning of Truth.* Cambridge: Harvard University Press, 1978.

———. "Remarks at the Peace Banquet." *The Atlantic Monthly,* December 1904. https://www.theatlantic.com/magazine/archive/1904/12/remarks-at-the-peace-banquet/307802/.

———. "The Will to Believe." In *The Will to Believe and Other Essays in Popular Philosophy,* by William James, 1–31. New York: Dover, 1956.

Johnson, Dominic. *God Is Watching You: How the Fear of God Makes Us Human.* Oxford: Oxford University Press, 2016.

Johnson, Wayne G. "Explaining Diversity in Moral Thought: A Theory." In *The Southern Journal of Philosophy* 26.1 (1988) 115–33.

———. "The Freight of God." In *The Existence of God: Essays from the Basic Issues Forum,* edited by John R. Jacobson and Robert Lloyd Mitchell, 29–51. Lewisten, ME: Edwin Mellen, 1988.

———. *Judging Jesus: World Religions' Answers to "Who Do People Say That I Am?"* New York: Hamilton, 2014.

———. "Psychological Egoism: *Noch Einmal.*" *Journal of Philosophical Research* 17 (1992) 239–64.

Juergensmeyer, Mark. *Terror in the Mind of God: The Global Rise of Religious Violence.* Berkeley, CA: University of California Press, 2001.

Kant, Immanuel. *Grounding for the Metaphysics of Morals.* Translated by J. W. Ellington. Indianapolis: Hackett, 1981.

Keith, Sir Arthur. *Evolution and Ethics.* New York: Putnam's, 1947.

Kierkegaard, Soren. *Sickness Unto Death*. Translated by Alastair Hannay. London: Penguin, 1989.

———. *Stages on Life's Way*. Edited and translated by Howard V. Hong and Edna H. Hong. Princeton, NJ: Princeton University Press, 1988.

King, Winston I. *In the Hope of Nibbana: The Ethics of Theravada Buddhism*. LaSalle, IL: Open Court, 1964.

Klemke, E. D., ed. *The Meaning of Life*. New York: Oxford University Press, 1981.

Krakauer, Jon. *Under the Banner of Heaven: A Story of a Violent Faith*. New York: Doubleday, 2003.

Lauren, Paul. *The Evolution of International Human Rights*. Philadelphia: University of Pennsylvania Press, 1998.

Leiter, Brian. "The Death of God and the Death of Morality." *The Monist* 102.3 (2019) 386–402.

Leiter, Brian, and Neil Sinhababu, eds. *Nietzsche and Morality*. Oxford: Clarendon, 2007.

Lifton, Robert. *The Life of the Self: Toward a New Psychology*. New York: Simon & Schuster, 1976.

MacIntyre, Alasdair. *After Virtue: A Study in Moral Theory*. Notre Dame, IN: University of Notre Dame Press, 1981.

———. *A Short History of Ethics*. New York: Macmillan, 1966.

———. *Three Rival Versions of Moral Inquiry*. Notre Dame, IN: Notre Dame University Press, 1990.

———. *Whose Justice? Which Rationality?* Notre Dame, IN: Notre Dame University Press, 1988.

Mackie, John. *Ethics: Inventing Right and Wrong*. New York: Penguin, 1977.

Marino, Gordon, ed. *Ethics: The Essential Writings*. New York: Random House, 2010.

Metzger, Bruce M., and Roland E. Murphy, eds. *The New Oxford Annotated Bible*. New York: Oxford University Press, 1991.

Mill, J. S. *Utilitarianism*. Edited by George Sher. Indianapolis: Hackett, 1979.

Mitchell, Basil. *Morality: Religious and Secular*. Oxford: Oxford University Press, 1980.

Mitsis, Phillip. "Epicureanism." In *Encyclopedia of Ethics*, 1:318.

Morison, James Dalton, comp. and ed. *Minister's Service Book*. New York: Harper, 1937.

Mullen, John Douglas. *Kierkegaard's Philosophy: Self Deception and Cowardice in the Present Age*. New York: New American Library, 1981.

Newman, J. H. *Minister's Service Book*. Compiled and edited by James Dalton Morrison. New York: Harper, 1937.

Nielsen, Kai. *Ethics Without God*. Buffalo, NY: Prometheus, 1973.

Nietzsche, Friedrich. *The Joyful Wisdom*. Translated by Thomas Common. London: Allen & Unwin, 1910.

Noss, D. S., and J. B. Noss. *A History of the World's Religions*. Upper Saddle River, NJ: Prentice Hall, 1994.

Nowell-Smith, P. H. *Ethics*. Baltimore, MD: Penguin, 1969.

Orend, Brian. *Human Rights: Concept and Content*. Peterborough, Canada: Broadview, 2002.

Paloutzian, Raymond. *Invitation to the Psychology of Religion*. 2nd ed. Boston: Allyn & Bacon, 1996.

Pascal, Blaise. *Pensees and Other Writings*. Translated by Honor Levi. New York: Oxford University Press, 1995.

BIBLIOGRAPHY

Parks, Sharon. *The Critical Years: Young Adults and the Search for Meaning, Faith, and Commitment*. San Francisco: HarperCollins, 1991.

Perry, Michael. *The Idea of Human Rights: Four Inquiries*. New York: Oxford University Press, 1998.

Plato. *Complete Works of Plato*. Edited with introduction and notes by John M. Cooper, edited in association with P. S. Hutchinson. Indianapolis: Hackett, 1997.

Plato. *Phaedo*. In *Complete Works of Plato*, edited by John Cooper, 49-100. Indianapolis: Hackett, 1992.

Prothero, Stephen. *American Jesus: How the Son of God Became a National Icon*. New York: Farrar, Straus & Giroux, 2003.

Putnam, Hilary. *Ethics Without Ontology*. Cambridge, MA: Harvard University Press, 2004.

Rachels, James. *The Elements of Moral Philosophy*. New York: Random House, 1986.

Rawls, John. *A Theory of Justice*. Cambridge, MA: Harvard University Press, 1971.

Rolston, Holmes, III. *Genes, Genesis, and God*. Cambridge: Cambridge University Press, 1999.

Rorty, Richard. *Philosophy and Social Hope*. London: Penguin, 1999.

Ruse, Michael, and Edward O. Wilson. "The Evolution of Ethics." *New Scientist* 17 (1985).

Russell, Bertrand. "A Free Man's Worship." In *The Meaning of Life*, edited by E. D. Klemke, 55-62. New York: Oxford University Press, 1981.

Sachs, Jonathan. *Morality: Restoring the Common Good in Divided Times*. New York: Basic, 2020.

Schiebe, Karl. *Beliefs and Values*. New York: Holt, Rinehart & Winston, 1970.

Schneewind, J. B., ed. *Reason, Ethics, and Society*. Chicago: Open Court, 1996.

Sher, George. ed. *Moral Philosophy: Selected Readings*. New York: Harcourt Brace Javonovich, 1987.

Shermer, Michael. *The Moral Arc: How Science and Reason Lead Humanity Toward Truth, Justice, and Freedom*. New York: Holt, 2015.

Sidgwick, Henry. *The Methods of Ethics*. New York: Dover, 1966.

———. *Outlines of the History of Ethics*. Boston: Beacon, 1960.

Singer, Peter. *The Expanding Circle: Ethics, Evolution, and Moral Progress*. Princeton, NJ: Princeton University Press, 1981,

———. *Practical Ethics*. 2nd ed. Cambridge: Cambridge University Press, 1993.

Smart, Ninian. *Beyond Ideology*. San Francisco: Harper & Row, 1981.

———. *Worldviews: Crosscultural Explorations of Human Beliefs*. New York: Scribner's, 1983.

Sober, E. *From a Biological Point of View*. Cambridge: Cambridge University Press, 1994.

Sober, E., and D. S. Wilson. *Unto Others: The Evolution and Psychology of Unselfish Behavior*. Cambridge, MA: Harvard University Press, 1988.

Stark, Rodney. *For the Glory of God*. Princeton, NJ: Princeton University Press, 2003.

Stout, Jeffrey. *Ethics after Babel: The Languages of Morals and Their Discontents*. Boston: Beacon, 1988.

———. *The Flight from Authority: Religion, Morality, and the Quest for Autonomy*. Notre Dame, IN: Notre Dame University Press, 1981.

Strauss, Leo. *Natural Right and History*. Chicago: University of Chicago Press, 1953.

Stumpf, S. E. *Socrates to Sartre*. New York: McGraw-Hill, 1982.

Taylor, Richard. *Ethics, Faith, and Reason*. Englewood Cliffs, NJ: Prentice-Hall, 1985.

———. *Good and Evil*. New York: Macmillan, 1970.

———. "The Meaning of Life." In *The Meaning of Life,* edited by E. D. Klemke, 141–50. New York: Oxford University Press, 1981.
Thilly, Frank, and Ledger Wood. *A History of Philosophy.* New York: Holt, Rinehart & Winston, 1963.
Thomas, George F., *Religious Philosophies of the West.* New York: Scribner's, 1965.
Thompson, Judith Jarvis. "Killing and Letting Die, and the Trolley Problems." *The Monist* 59 (1976) 204–17.
Tillich, Paul. *The Courage to Be.* New Haven: Yale University Press, 1952.
———. *Love, Power, and Justice.* New York: Oxford University Press, 1954.
———. *The Protestant Era.* Chicago: The University of Chicago Press, 1957.
———. *Systematic Theology.* 3 vols. Chicago: The University of Chicago Press, 1963.
Tolstoy, Leo. "Religion and Morality." In *Leo Tolstoy: Selected Essays.* Translated by Aylmer Maude, selected and introduced by Ernest J. Simmens. New York: Modern Library, 1964.
———. *War and Peace.* Translated by Louise and Aylmer Maud. New York: Norton, 1966.
Waley, Arthur. *Three Was of Thought in Ancient China.* Garden City, NY: Doubleday, 1939.
Warnock, G. J. *Contemporary Moral Philosophy.* London: Macmillan, 1967.
———. *The Object of Morality.* London: Methuen, 1971.
Whale, J. S. *The Protestant Tradition.* Cambridge: Cambridge University Press, 1955.
White, Michael, and John Gribbin. *Einstein: A Life in Science.* New York: Dutton, 1993.
White, R. E. O. *Christian Ethics: The Historical Development.* Changing Continuity of Christian Ethics 2. Atlanta, GA: John Knox, 1981.
Williams, Bernard. *Ethics and the Limits of Philosophy.* Cambridge, MA: Harvard University Press, 1985.
Wilson, Edward O. *On Human Nature.* Cambridge, MA: Harvard University Press, 1978.
———. *Sociobiology: The New Synthesis.* Cambridge, MA: Harvard University Press, 1975.
Wilson, James Q. *The Moral Sense.* New York: Simon & Schuster, 1993.
Wright, Robert. *The Evolution of God.* New York: Little Brown, 2009.

Index

absolutism, 104, 147
aesthete, 36
aesthetic stage, 35
Alexander, R. D., 20, 162, 164
altruism, 131,169
Anscombe, G. E. M., 141
Aquinas, Thomas, 64–68, 143
Aristotle, 9, 58–62, 64
atomists, 47
Augustine, St., 62–64, 108, 140, 143
autonomy, 108

Baier, Kurt, 134, 135
Becker, Ernest, 38, 40
Bellah, Robert, 113
Bentham, Jeremy, 83, 113, 143
Bhagavad-Gita, 115, 119
broad theory, 3, 11
Buddha, 108
Buddhism, 195

Calvin, John, 143
Camus, Albert, 36
Carvaka, 50
cat—hold model, 101
categorical imperative, 78
Cicero, 140
class struggle, 89, 90
cosmic meaning, 31
cultural relativism, 146

Darwin, Charles, 162, 163, 171
Dawkins, Richard, 166

Dennett, Daniel, 163
deontological ethics, 14
despair, 36, 37
determinism, 88, 156
determinism, hard, 155
determinism, soft, 155
DuCasse, C. J., 127
duty, 78, 129

egoism, psychological, 172, 173
egoistic hedonism, 48
Einstein, Albert, 154
emotive theory, 17
Epicurus, 3, 9, 30, 47, 49
ethical absolutism, 146, 150
ethical egoism, 153
ethical relativism, 146, 147
ethical stage, 36
Eudaemnism, 61
evolution, 162, 164
evolutionary psychology, 161

Fall, The, 36
Feinberg, Joel, 126, 172
Fox, George, 118
Frankena, Wm., 131, 136
free will, 154, 156
Freud, Sigmund, 143
fulfillment, 3, 31

Gandhi, M., 119
Gauthier, David, 133
Geertz, Clifford, 5, 97

INDEX

Gert, Bernard, 180
God, death of, 91, 94
Green, Ronald, 141
guilt, 2

Halverson, W. H., 177
happiness, 67
Harris, Sam, 177
Hemingway, Ernest, 32
heteronomy, 108
Hinduism, 44, 175
Hobbes, Thomas, 66–71, 172
Hudson, W. D., 5, 20, 130
Hume, David, 72–76, 173

immortality, 53
intuitions, 135
is—ought distinction, 173

Jains, 119, 175
James, William, 5, 21, 110, 145
Jefferson, Thomas, 124, 126, 143
Johnson, Dominic, 143, 176
Johnson, Wayne G., 177
justice, 138

Kant, Immanuel, 76–82
Key, Francis Scott, 110
Kierkegaard, Soren, 2, 34
kin selection, 168
King, M. L., Jr., 119

law, divine, 66, 105–7
law, natural, 65, 102, 124
Laws (Plato), 51, 55
Leiter, Brian, 178
Leviticus, 118
Lifton, Robert, 178
Locke, John, 124, 143
love, 63, 117
Lucretius, 30
lying, 79

MacIntyre, Alasdair, 113, 127, 138, 140
Mackie, John, 133
Maimonides, 58, 143
Malthus, Thomas, 162

Marx, Karl, 87–91
master morality, 92
materialism, historical, 88
materialism, ontological, 88
Matthew, Gospel of, 110
meaning of life, 31
meaninglessness, 43
Mill, J. S., 83–87, 125, 143
Monod, J., 32
monkey—hold model, 101
moral nihilist, 151
moral point of view, 27, 136
morality, point of, 20, 26
mortality, 39, 41
Muhammad, 117
Muslims, 117

naturalism, 7
Nazi, 120
neighbor, 117, 118
Nietzsche, F., 9, 91–94
nihilism, 32
nihilist, moral, 151
Noss, D. S., 178

ontological materialism, 7
our moral setting, 23

Parks, Sharon, 181
Pascal, B., 40
philosopher king, 57
Plato, 9, 41, 50–58, 143
predestination, 102
Prime Mover, 59
principle of utility, 84
projection theory of ethics, 18
Protagoras, 16, 148
Prothero, Stephen, 181
psychological egoism, 172, 173
psychological hedonism, 83

Quakers, 118, 119

rational egoism, 112, 128
reciprocal altruism, 169
reincarnation, 41
religious stage, 37

190

Republic, 57
rights, civil, 122
rights, human, 70, 121, 122–24
rights, legal, 121
rights, natural, 70
Rokeach, Milton, 38
Romans, letter to, 30
Rorty, Richard, 125
Ruse, Michael, 164
Russell, Bertrand, 34

sanctions, 12, 141
Sartre, J. P., 94–96
sea turtle model, 100
self interest, 129
self referential, 130, 131
Selfish Gene, 165
selfishness, 130. 167
Shakers, 175
Sidgwick, Henry, 111, 112
Singer, Peter, 136
Sisyphus, 31, 33
situation ethics, 104
slavery, 57, 61
Smart, Ninian, 114
Sober, E., 182
Society of Friends, 119
sociobiology, 161
Socrates, 139
soul, 53, 60

St. Paul, 117, 140
state, 68, 116
Stoics, 139
Stumph, Samuel E., 178
symbolic immortality, 42
sympathy, 75, 168

Taylor, Richard, 46, 132, 142
teleological ethics, 13
temporal meaning, 33
theonomy, 108
theories, 10
Thilly, Frank, 178
Thomas, George F., 179
Tillich, Paul, 108
Tolstoy, Leo, 46, 154
tribalism, 111, 113, 116
trolley problem, 2

universalizing, 137, 141
utilitarianism, 84

Whale, J. S., 179
White, R. E. O., 180
will to power, 96
Wilson, D. S., 182
Wilson, E. O., 164
worldviews, 6, 99
Wood, Ledger, 178

CPSIA information can be obtained
at www.ICGtesting.com
Printed in the USA
BVHW091405160222
629171BV00003B/9